C ELEMENTS OF
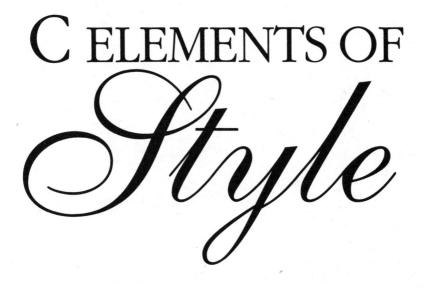

C ELEMENTS OF *Style*

STEVE OUALLINE

The Programmer's Style Manual for

Elegant C and C++ Programs

M&T Books
A Division of M&T Publishing, Inc.
411 Borel Avenue, Suite 100
San Mateo, CA 94402

Limits of Liability and Disclaimer of Warranty
The Author and Publisher of this book have used their best efforts in preparing the book and the programs contained in it. These efforts include the development, research, and testing of the theories and programs to determine their effectiveness.

The Author and Publisher make no warranty of any kind, expressed or implied, with regard to these programs or the documentation contained in this book. The Author and Publisher shall not be liable in any event for incidental or consequential damages in connection with, or arising out of, the furnishing, performance, or use of these programs.

All brand names, trademarks, and registered trademarks are the property of their respective holders.

Library of Congress Cataloging-in-Publication Data

Oualline, Steve.
C Elements of Style: the programmers guide to developing well written C and C++
programs / Steve Oualline.
     p. cm.
Includes bibliographical references and index.
ISBN 1-55851-291-8
1. C (Computer program language) 2. C++ (Computer program language) I. Title
QA76.73.C153083   1992   92-33734
005.13'3--dc20   CIP

95   94   93 92   4 3 2 1

Technical Editor: Michael Swaine   **Cover Design:** Lauren Smith Design
Project Editor: Meredith Ittner   **Art Director:** Margaret Horoszko
Copy Editor: Anne Kandra   **Page Layout:** Stacey L. Evans

Contents

Why This Book Is for You

This book is for programmers who create, edit, modify, and maintain C and C++ code and who want their programs to be easily read and maintained by others. The ability to read and maintain a program has become increasingly important as programs live longer and grow in size and complexity.

This book is for programmers who recognize that style is an important part of modern programming and that good style improves not only the readability of a program but its reliability.

Finally, this book is for programmers who want to avoid the little traps and pitfalls that occur in programming C and C++ and prevent the bugs that can develop. The rules presented in this book help you understand and avoid these problems.

If you want to write better C or C++ code, this book is for you.

Introduction

This book is for all those programmers who have slaved till two in the morning trying to find a bug in someone else's code.

It is not intended to be a stuffy shelf reference brought out to resolve debates. While programming style rules and guidelines may be set at the team level, it's the individual programmer who faces the particular problems of style. Facing those problems, the programmer wants a book at hand that presents clear rules based on years of experience of many programmers, that is supported by the reasoning behind the rules, and that shows when the rules can be violated intelligently. That's the kind of book I want at my elbow when I'm programming, and it's the kind of book I hope I have written.

As the size and complexity of programs skyrocket, more and more programmers are realizing that good, clear programming style is an absolute necessity. Good style helps make programs more reliable and easier to maintain. And these qualities are vital in a world where the average size, age, and complexity of software systems are constantly growing.

The programming style set forth in this book is designed to serve just two goals: readability and reliability.

Readability is essential today because programmers no longer spend most of their time writing code. Most of their time is spent maintaining and enhancing existing programs. That makes readability a requirement.

Comments are the most effective tool for making code readable. The style described in this book makes extensive and thoughtful use of comments.

Reliability is enhanced by using a defensive programming style—one that limits the ability of the C compiler to cause you problems. Many of the rules in this book are designed to help you avoid the hidden gotchas lurking in the language.

Beyond the goals of readability and reliability, style is superfluous. It can even get in the way of writing clear and concise programs. An example of style run amuck is the Federal Register: 100,000 pages of precise legal specifications written in a highly formal, regulated style that no one understands.

Too much style is bad style.

How This Book's Style Was Developed

This book describes a programming style I've developed over the years by working on thousands of lines of C code. I've spent a lot of time going through other people's code, and I've seen the good, the bad, and the ugly. In order to understand what's going on I make notes, but rather than put these notes on paper, I put them in the code, in comments. This is because I can't read my own handwriting, but mostly it is to make sure that I keep the code and the notes together.

After doing this for a while I noticed that my commenting tended to follow some patterns, and as I studied these patterns, they developed into the commenting style presented in this book. Also, in going through other people's code I have had the opportunity to examine their styles. Over the years, I have seen a lot of different approaches to programming style. Some have worked, some haven't. The good ideas I kept and have included in this book. Some of the bad ideas are here too, as examples of what not to do.

The other way I've developed this book's style is by making mistakes. Whenever I screw up, I ask myself, "Why did I make this error? Is there any way I could change my programming style to eliminate the possibility of that kind of error—or in other words, to make my programming less risky?" My goal has been to come up with a set of rules to limit the number of things that I have to keep track of.

Another way to put it is that I do a lot of thinking so that I don't have to do a lot of thinking. For example, some care must be taken when using the operator ++ inside an assignment statement. It can lead to trouble. But I don't have to decide whether or not it's safe to combine ++ and assignments if I always put ++ in a separate statement. That way I have one less thing to worry about.

Another example: C has 21 precedence rules (<< comes before ||, etc.). I can't memorize all these rules, so I have learned a simple subset:

1) * % / come before + and -
2) Put () around everything else

This subset is easy to memorize and will increase the simplicity and reliability of your programs. (You'll make fewer mistakes if you use it.) And even if you know all 21 precedence rules, don't be too smug. The real question is not how good your memory is, but how many of the rules you can safely assume that another programmer reading your code ten years from now will have memorized. Stick to the subset.

What's In This book

The first part of this book describes a set of rules for good C style and discusses the reasons behind the rules. Part I is divided into the following chapters:

Chapter 1 Discusses program organization and commenting techniques.

Chapter 2 Describes the comments that go at the beginning of a program and module as well as high-level module design.

Chapter 3 Focuses on variable names and how to comment a declaration statement.

Chapter 4 Gives you some guidelines on how to format the body of your code.

Chapter 5 Goes through the format and design of each type of C statement.

Chapter 6 Describes how to use the preprocessor and presents a set of rules to keep you from shooting yourself in the foot with it.

Chapter 7 Details the special style rules needed for C++.

Chapter 8 Describes Makefile design.

Chapter 9 Discusses user-friendly programming.

Finally, for those of you who want a concise set of rules without all the discussion, Part II is a style manual. A complete list of rules by chapter is presented in Appendix B.

Throughout this book we have used the Letter Gothic font for C code and program examples. Bold is used for C keywords and italic for file names and any code that appears within the body of the text.

I wish to thank the hundreds of programmers whose code I used in making this book. I also want to thank my editor Michael Swaine for the fine job he did on this manuscript, Meredith Ittner for taking care of a thousand and one details, and finally Brenda McLaughlin deserves a special thanks for the work she did in getting this book ready for press in record time.

## PART I

Rules for C Style

## CHAPTER 1

Style and Program Organization

A program is a detailed set of instructions read by both a human and a machine. The computer reads only the code, while the human concentrates on the comments.

Good style pertains to both parts of a program. Well-designed, well-written code not only makes effective use of the computer, it also contains carefully constructed comments to help humans understand it. Well-designed, well-written code is a joy to debug, maintain, and enhance.

Good programming style begins with the effective organization of code. By using a clear and consistent organization of the components of your programs, you make them more efficient, readable, and maintainable.

Program Organization

Good computer programs are organized much like good books. This can be seen especially well with technical books, in which the structure is very clear.

People have been writing books for hundreds of years, and during that time they have discovered how to organize the material to efficiently present their ideas. Standards have emerged. For example, if I asked you when this book was copyrighted, you would turn to the title page. That's where the copyright notice is always located.

The same goes for code. In fact, we can make the parallels quite explicit.

Any technical book can be analyzed into standard components. So can any program. These components correspond quite closely as the following table shows.

Book	Program
Book	**Program**
Title Page	Heading
Table of Contents	Table of Contents
Chapter	Module
Section	Function
Paragraph	Conceptual Block
Sentence	Statement
Word	Variable
Index	Cross Reference
Glossary	Glossary

These components really do serve the same purposes.

- **Title Page**

  A book's title page contains the name of the book, the author, and the publisher. On the reverse of the title page is the copyright page, where you find things like the printing history and Library of Congress information.

  At the beginning of every well-documented program is a section known as the heading. It is, in effect, the title page of the program. The heading consists of a set of boxed comments that include the name of the program, the author, copyright, usage, and other important information. The heading comments are fully discussed in Chapter 2. The program's heading also includes **#define** and **#undef** for any conditional compilation symbols (see Chapter 6) and **#include** directives.

- **Table of Contents**

  Every technical book has a table of contents. It lists the location of all the chapters and major headings, and serves as a road map to the rest of the book.

  A program should have a table of contents as well, listing the location of each function. This is difficult and tedious to produce by hand, however it can be produced quite easily by a number of readily available tools, as discussed later in this chapter.

- **Chapters**

Technical books are divided into chapters, each one covering a single subject. Generally, each chapter in a technical book consists of a chunk of material that a reader can read in one sitting, although this is not a rule: Donald Knuth's highly regarded 624-page *Fundamental Algorithms* (Addison-Wesley, Reading, MA, 1968) contains only two chapters.

Similarly, a program is divided into modules, each a single file containing a set of functions designed to do some specific job. A short program may consist of just one module, while larger programs can contain 10, 20, or more. Module design is further discussed later in this chapter.

- **Sections**

Each chapter in a technical book is typically divided into several sections. A section covers a smaller body of information than a chapter. Sections in this book are identified by section heads in bold letters, making it easy for a reader to scan a chapter for a particular subject.

Just as a book chapter can contain several sections, a program module may contain several functions. A function is a set of instructions designed to perform a single focused task. A function should be short enough that a programmer can easily understand the entire function.

- **Index**

A technical book should have a good index that lists every important subject or keyword in the book and the pages on which it can be found. The index is extremely important in a technical book because it provides quick access to specific information.

A program of any length should have a cross reference, which lists the program variables and constants, along with the line numbers where they are used. A cross reference serves as an index for the program, aiding the programmer in finding variables and determining what they do. A cross reference can be generated automatically by one of the many cross reference tools, such as *xref*, *cref*, etc.

- **Glossary**

  A glossary is particularly important in a technical book. Each technical profession has its own language, and this is especially true in computer programming (e.g., set COM1 to 1200,8,N,1 to avoid PE and FE errors). A reader can turn to the glossary to find the meaning of these special words. Every C program uses its own set of variables, constants, and functions. These names change from program to program, so a glossary is essential. Producing one by hand is impractical, but as you'll see later in this chapter, with a little help from some strategically placed comments, you can easily generate a glossary automatically.

Rule 1-1:

Organize programs for readability, just as you would expect an author to organize a book.

Automatic Generation of Program Documentation

Some of the program components described above can be generated automatically. Consider the table of contents, for example. On UNIX systems, the *ctags* program will create such a table. Also, there is a public domain program, called *cpr*, that does the job for both DOS and UNIX.

A cross reference can also be generated automatically by one of the many cross reference tools, such as *xref*, *cref*, etc. However, you can also generate a cross reference one symbol at a time. Suppose you want to find out where *total_count* is located. The command *grep* searches files for a string, so typing:

```
grep -n total_count *.c
```

produces a list of every use of *total_count* in all the C files. (The *-n* tells *grep* to print line numbers.)

The command *grep* is available both on UNIX systems and on DOS with Turbo-C.

Also in UNIX, the command:

```
vi `grep -l total_count *.c`
```

invokes the *vi* editor to list the files that contain the word *total_count*. Then you can use the *vi* search command to locate *total_count* within a file. The commands next (*:next*) and rewind (*:rew*) will flip through the files. See your *vi* and UNIX manuals for more details.

Turbo-C has a version of *grep* built in to the Integrated Develop Environment (IDE). By using the command Alt-Space you can bring up the tools menu, then select *grep* and give it a command line, and the program will generate a list of references in the message window. The file corresponding to the current message window line is displayed in the edit window. Going up or down in the message changes the edit window. With these commands, you can quickly locate every place a variable is used.

You can also partially automate the process of building a glossary, which is a time-consuming task if performed entirely by hand. The trick is to put a descriptive comment after each variable declaration. That way, when the maintenance programmer wants to know what *total_count* means, all he or she has to do is look up the first time *total_count* in mentioned in the cross reference, locate that line in the program, and read:

```
int total_count;/* Total number of items in all classes */
```

So we have a variable (*total_count*) and its definition: "Total number of items in all classes"—in other words, a glossary entry.

Module Design

A module is a set of functions that perform related operations. A simple program consists of one file; i.e., one module. More complex programs are built of several modules.

Modules have two parts: the public interface, which gives a user all the information necessary to use the module; and the private section, which actually does the work.

Another analogy to books is helpful here. Consider the documentation for a piece of equipment like a laser printer. This typically consists of two manuals: the Operator's Guide and the Technical Reference Manual.

The Operator's Guide describes how to use the laser printer. It includes information like what the control panel looks like, how to put in paper, and how to change the toner. It does not cover *how* the printer works.

A user does not need to know what goes on under the covers. As long as the printer does its job, it doesn't matter how it does it. When the printer stops working, the operator calls in a technician, who uses the information in the Technical Reference Manual to make repairs. This manual describes how to disassemble the machine, test the internal components, and replace broken parts.

The public interface of a module is like an Operator's Guide. It tells the programmer and the computer how to use the module. The public interface of a module is called the "header file." It contains data structures, function definitions, and **#define** constants, which are needed by anyone using the module. The header file also contains a set of comments that tells a programmer how to use the module.

The private section, the actual code for the module, resides in the *.c* file. A programmer who uses the module never needs to look into this file. Some commercial products even distribute their modules in object form only, so *nobody* can look in the private section.

Rule 1-2:

> Divide each module up into a public part (what's needed to use the module) and a private part (what's needed to get the job done). The public part goes into a *.h* file while the private part goes into a *.c* file.

Libraries and Other Module Groupings

A library is a collection of generally useful modules combined into a special object file.

Libraries present a special problem: How do you present the public information for a library? Do you use a single header file, multiple header files for the individual modules, or some other method?

There is no one answer. Each method has its advantages and disadvantages.

Multiple header files

Because a library is a collection of modules, you could use a collection of header files to interface with the outside world. The advantage to this is that a program brings in only the function and data definitions it needs, and leaves out what it doesn't use.

The X-Windows system, for example, has a different header file for each module (called a tool kit in X-language).

A typical X-Windows program contains code that looks like this:

```
#include <X11/Intrinsic.h>
#include <X11/Shell.h>
#include <Xm/Xm.h>
#include <Xm/Label.h>
#include <Xm/RowColumn.h>
#include <Xm/PushB.h>
#include <Xm/Separator.h>
#include <Xm/BulletinB.h>
#include <Xm/CascadeB.h>
```

As you can see, this can result in a lot of **#include**s. One of the problems with this system is that it is very easy to forget one of the **#include** statements. Also, it is possible to have redundant **include**s. For example, suppose the header file *Xm/Label.h* requires *Xm/Separator.h* and contains an internal **#include** for it, but the program itself also includes it. In this case, the file is included twice, which makes extra, unnecessary work for the compiler.

Also, it is very easy to forget which include files are needed and which to leave out. I've often had to go through a cycle of compile and get errors, figure out which include file is missing, and compile again.

Therefore, the advantages of being compact must be balanced against the disadvantages of being complex and difficult to use.

One header does all

One way of avoiding the problems of multiple header files is to throw everything into a single, big header file. Microsoft Windows uses this approach. A typical Windows program contains the line:

```
#include <windows.h>
```

This is much simpler than the multiple include file approach taken by X-Windows. Also, there is no problem with loading a header file twice because there is only one file and only one **#include** statement.

The problem is that this file is 3,500 lines long, so even short 10-line modules bring in 3,500 lines of include file. This make compilation slower. Borland and Microsoft have tried to get around this problem by introducing "pre-compiled" headers, but it still takes time to compile Windows programs.

Mixed approach

Borland's Turbo Vision library (TV) uses a different method. The programmer puts **#define** statements in the code to tell the TV header which functions will be used. This is followed by one **#include** directive.

```
#define Uses_TRect
#define Uses_TStatusLine
#define Uses_TStatusDef
#define Uses_TStatusItem

#include <tv.h>
```

The file *tv.h* brings in additional include files as needed. (The **#define**s determine what is needed.) One advantage over multiple include files is that the files are included in the proper order, which eliminates redundant includes.

This system has another advantage in that only the data that's needed is brought in, so compilation is faster. The disadvantage is that if you forget to put in the correct **#define** statements, your program won't compile. So while being faster than the all-in-one strategy, it is somewhat more complex.

Program Aesthetics

A properly designed program is easy to read and understand.

Part of what makes books readable is good paragraphing. Books are broken up into paragraphs and sentences. A sentence forms one complete thought, and multiple sentences on a single subject form a paragraph.

Code paragraphs

Similarly, a C program consists of statements, and multiple statements on the same subject form a conceptual block. Since "conceptual block" is not a recognized technical term, you may just as well call them paragraphs. In this book, paragraphs are separated from each other by a blank line. You can separate paragraphs in C in the same way.

Omitting paragraphs in code creates ugly, hard-to-read programs. If you've ever tried reading a paper without paragraphing, you realize how easy it is to get lost. Paragraph-less programming tends to cause the programmer to get lost:

```
/* Poor programming style */
void display(void)
{
    int start, finish;      /* Start, End of display range */
    char line[80];          /* Input line for events */
    printf("Event numbers ? ");
    start = -1;
    finish = -1;
    fgets(line, sizeof(line), stdin);
    sscanf(line,"%d %d", &start, &finish);
    if (start == -1)
        return;
    if (!valid(finish))
        finish = start;
    if (valid(start))
        display2(start, finish);
}
```

Now, see how much better the same code looks after adding some white space to separate the function into paragraphs:

```
/* good programming style */
void display(void)
{
    int start, finish;      /* Start, End of display range */
    char line[80];          /* Input line for events */
```

```
        printf("Event numbers ? ");
        start = -1;
        finish = -1;
        fgets(line, sizeof(line), stdin);
        sscanf(line,"%d %d", &start, &finish);

        if (start == -1)
            return;

        if (!valid(finish))
            finish = start;

        if (valid(start))
            display2(start, finish);
}
```

Note that the paragraphs here are not defined by the syntax of the language, but by the semantics of the program. Statements are grouped together if they belong together logically. That judgement is made by the programmer.

Rule 1-3:
Use white space to break a function into paragraphs.

Statements
Good paragraphing improves the aesthetics, hence the readability, of a program. But there are also aesthetic issues at the level of the sentence; or in C, the statement. A statement expresses a single thought, idea, or operation. Putting each statement on a line by itself makes the statement stand out and reserves the use of indentations for showing program structure.

```
/* Avoid this style of programming */
void dump_regs()
{
    {int d_reg_indtf("d%d 0x%x\n",
        d_reg_index,d_reg[d_reg_index]);}
```

```
{int a_reg_index;for(a_reg_index=0;a_reg_index<7;
a_reg_index++)printf("a%d 0x%x\n",
     a_reg_index, a_reg[a_reg_index]);}
}
```

Figuring out this code is like extracting a fossil from a rock formation. You must take out your hammer and chip at it again and again until something coherent emerges. This kind of programming obscures the control flow of the program. It hides statement beginnings and endings and provides no paragraph separations.

Simply reformatting this code gives us a clearer understanding of what it does.

```
/* Better style */
void dump_regs()
{
    {
        int d_reg_index;

        for(d_reg_index = 0; d_reg_index < 7; d_reg_index++)
            printf("d%d 0x%x\n",
                d_reg_index, d_reg[d_reg_index]);
    }

    {
        int a_reg_index;

        for(a_reg_index = 0; a_reg_index < 7; a_reg_index++)
            printf("a%d 0x%x\n",
                a_reg_index, a_reg[a_reg_index]);
    }
}
```

(Better yet, add comments after the *d_reg_index* and *a_reg_index* declarations to explain the variables.)

Rule 1-4:

Put each statement on a line by itself.

In clearly written English there are limits on the optimum length of a sentence. We've all suffered through the sentence that runs on and on, repeating itself over and over; or, through a structure whose complexity demonstrates more the confusion than the cleverness of the author (although it should be noted that, as in the present example, a demonstration of confusion can be the whole point), just get all bollixed up.

Likewise, a clearly written C statement should not go on forever. Complex statements can easily be divided into smaller, more concise statements. For example:

```
/* Poor practice */
ratio = (load * stress - safety_margin -
        fudge_factor) / (length * width * depth -
        shrinkage);

/* Better */
top = (load * stress - safety_margin - fudge_factor);
bottom = (length * width * depth - shrinkage);

ratio = top / bottom;
```

Rule 1-5:

Avoid very long statements. Use two shorter statements instead.

Some of the rules in this chapter will be repeated later in other contexts. All of this chapter's rules are summarized here.

Rules

1-1. Organize programs for readability, just as you would expect an author to organize a book.

1-2. Divide each module up into a public part (what's needed to use the module) and a private part (what's needed to get the job done). The public part goes into a .h file while the private part goes into a .c file.

1-3. Use white space to break a function into paragraphs.

1-4. Put each statement on a line by itself.

1-5. Avoid very long statements. Use two shorter statements instead.

## CHAPTER 2

File Basics, Comments, and Program Headings

To program some of the very early computers, programmers had to rewire the machine. The programmers got a large circuit board called a plug board, which was filled with little holes where they plugged in wires to create the program. Once they had programmed the board, they slid it into the computer and ran the program.

Computers soon evolved to the point where programmers could program them in text. They typed their program on a machine that output punched cards, dropped the thick deck of cards into the card reader, and the computer did the rest. Editing the program was as simple as replacing cards, but woe be to the programmer who dropped the program and scattered the cards.

Today we use text editors, which are certainly an improvement over punched cards and plug boards, but they do have their limitations. Knowing these limitations can help you to write code that will always be readable.

File Basics

C can accept files of almost any size, but there are some practical limitations. The longer a file, the more time and effort it takes to edit and print it. Most editors tend to get a bit slow when the file size gets to be more than about 3,000 lines. Keep yours within this limit.

Rule 2-1:

Keep programs files to no longer than about 2,000 to 3,000 lines.

Not only are there length limitations, but width limits as well. The old punch cards contained 80 columns. Because of that, most terminals and printers at the time were limited to 80 columns. This limitation has carried over to present-day computers. For example, the PC screen is only 80 columns wide.

Long lines can be a problem in programming. Many printers truncate lines that are too long, resulting in listings that look like this:

```
result = draw_line(last_x, last_y, next_x, next_y, line_style, end_style,
```

The code that fell off the right side is referred to as mystery code. So you need to limit the width of your program files to 80 characters. Actually, you need a slightly smaller limit. Program printers such as cpr print line numbered listings. Line numbers take up space, so a better limit, and one with enough history to be taken seriously, is 72 characters.

Rule 2-2:

Keep all lines in your program files down to 72 characters or fewer.

Early terminals had fixed tabs. Every eight characters you had a tab stop whether you liked it or not. You couldn't change them since they were built into the machine. This fixed tab size became an industry standard that is still in force today. If you type a file containing tabs under UNIX or DOS, the tabs come out every eight characters.

Many editors allow you to set your own tab stops. If you are programming in C with an indention size of 4, it is convenient to set the tab stop in your editor to 4. That way, to indent all you have to do is hit the Tab key. The problem with is that your tab setting is non-standard. If someone else edits your program, they won't know about your tabs and will assume that your code is indented strangely. Also, many printing programs and other programs default to a tab size of 8. Some, like DOS, can't be changed.

Note that tab size and indentation level are two different things. It is perfectly acceptable to use a tab size of 8 and an indentation level of 4. You would then use four spaces to reach the first level of indentation, a tab to reach the second, and so on.

Rule 2-3:

Use 8-character tab stops.

Finally, there is the character set. There are 95 printing characters in the standard ASCII set. The PC extended this set to include foreign characters and a line drawing set. It is possible to use the PC character set to draw interesting shapes, like the following example:

```
/************************************************
* Boxes look like                              *
*          ┌─────────────────────────┐         *
*          │                         │         *
*          │                         │         *
*          │                         │         *
*          └─────────────────────────┘         *
************************************************/
```

This makes for a nice picture on the screen, but what happens when you try to print it out? Most printers don't understand the PC character set, so you can easily get something that looks like this:

```
/************************************************
* Boxes look like                              *
*          LQQQQQQQQQQQQQQQQQQQQQQQQQL          *
*          M                         M          *
*          M                         M          *
*          M                         M          *
*          LQQQQQQQQQQQQQQQQQQQQQQQQQL          *
************************************************/
```

Worse, if this program is ported to another machine, such as a UNIX system, no one will understand the funny characters.

Rule 2-4:
> Use only the 95 standard ASCII characters in your programs. Avoid exotic characters.

The Comment

Well-written code can help a programmer understand what is going on, but the best form of communication is the comment. Comments are used to explain everything. Without comments, a programmer has to go through the long and painful process of decrypting the program to figure out what the heck it does.

The comment can convey a variety of information, including program design, coding details, tricks, traps, and sometimes even jokes. There are many types of comments, from important ones that you want make sure the programmer doesn't miss to explanations of the tiniest details.

The author of a book has the advantage of typesetting devices. Important information can be set in **BIG BOLD LETTERS**, or words can be *emphasized* with italics.

The programmer, on the other hand, is limited to a single size, single face, monospaced font and personal imagination. Over the years a lot of imagination has been used to make up for the limitations of the medium.

Rule 2-5:

> Include a heading comment at the beginning of each file that explains the file.

The following program illustrates a variety of commenting styles collected over the years from many different sources.

```
/*********************************************************
 * This is a boxed comment.  The box draws attention     *
 * to it.  This type of comment is used for program,     *
 * module and function headings.                         *
 *                                                       *
 * What to put in this box is discussed later.           *
 *********************************************************/
#include <stdio.h>

/* >>>>>>>>> Major Section Marker <<<<<<<<<< */

/* ——— Minor Section Marker ——— */

static int count = 0;    /* A simple end of line comment */
```

FILE BASICS, COMMENTS, AND PROGRAM HEADINGS

```c
/* This was an end of line comment that grew too long */
static int total = 0;


/**********************************************************
 **********************************************************
 ********** Warning:  This is a very important **********
 ********** message.  If the programmer misses **********
 ********** it, the program might crash and    **********
 ********** burn.  (Gets your attention,       **********
 ********** doesn't it?)                        **********
 **********************************************************
 **********************************************************/
main(void)
{
    /* This is an in-line comment */

    total++;

    /*
     * This is a longer in-line comment.
     * Because it is so verbose it is split into two lines.
     */
    return (0);
}
```

Other types of comments include:

```c
/*———————————————————*\
 * Another box style        *
\*———————————————————*/


/*
 *       * ============== *
 *       * Section Header *
 *       * ============== *
 *
 * This is a sentence with **one** word emphasized.
 */
```

Graphics

Computers are becoming more and more graphically oriented. Screen layouts, windowing systems, and games all require sophisticated graphics. It's not possible to put graphic comments into a program yet, but you can make a good attempt by using ASCII line art.

A typical screen layout comment might look like this:

```
/**********************************************************
 * Format of address menu                                 *
 *                                                        *
 *       <-- MENU_WIDTH ------->      MENU_HEIGHT          *
 *       +---------------------+                  ^       *
 *       | Name:_____  |<-- NAME_LINE     |       *
 *       | Address:_____  |<-- ADDR_LINE     |       *
 *       | City_____  |<-- CITY_LINE     |       *
 *       | State:___  Zip:____ |<-- STATE_LINE    |       *
 *       +---------------------+                  V       *
 *         ^           ^                                  *
 *         |           |                                  *
 *         |           + - ZIP_X                          *
 *         + -- BLANK_X                                   *
 **********************************************************/
```

Even with the crude drawing tools in the 95 standard ASCII characters, you can produce a recognizable picture. This type of comment actually conveys graphically the relationships among the constants shown.

Packing bits

If you do I/O programming, you know that hardware designers like to pack a lot of functions into a single byte. For example, the serial I/O chip that controls the COM ports on a PC contains a variety of packed registers.

Mode	Break		Parity		Stop	Stop	Bits

These registers are documented in the chip's data sheet. Unfortunately, most programmers don't carry around a complete set of data sheets, so it is very useful to copy the register specification into the program.

For example, the following line control register specification:

```
Parity:
        000 —   No parity
        001 —   Odd Parity/No Check
        010 —   Even Parity/No Check
        011 —   High Bit always set
        100 —   Odd Parity/Check Incoming characters
        101 —   Even Parity/Check Incoming characters
        110 —   Undefined
        111 —   High Bit always Clear

Stop Bits:
        00 —    1 Stop Bit
        01 —    1.5 Stop Bits
        10 —    2 Stop bits
        11 —    Undefined
```

turns into this:

```
/*************************************************************
 * Line Control Register                                     *
 *      for the PC's COM ports                               *
 *                                                           *
 *      76543210                                             *
 *      XXXXXXX                                              *
 *      ^^^^^^++—- Number of data bits                       *
 *      |||||+——- Number of stop bits                       *
 *      ||+++—— Parity control                              *
 *      |+———- Send Break                                   *
 *      +——— Mode control                                   *
 *************************************************************/
```

27

Letting the Editor Help You

Most editors have a macro of abbreviation features that make it quick and easy to create boxed comments.

If you use the UNIX editor vi, you can put the following in your *.exrc* file to define two abbreviations:

```
:abbr #b /*********************************************
:abbr #e *********************************************/
```

When you type *#b*, the editor changes it to a beginning box, while typing *#e* creates an ending comment.

On the PC, there is Borland's C++ compiler, which comes with a macro file named *CMACROS.TEM*. These macros must be installed using the *TEMC* command. Type:

```
TEMC cmacros.tem tcconfig.tc
```

These macros are a bit limited, however, and you might want to edit them before using them in production.

Beginning Comment Block

The first two questions a programmer should ask when confronting a strange program are "What is it?" and "What does it do?" Heading comments should answer both questions.

The top of a program serves as a sort of title page and abstract. It briefly describes the program and provides vital information about it.

Here, the heading comments are boxed. This not only makes them stand out, but it easily identifies them as containing important and generally useful information. The first line of the heading block contains the name of the program and a short description of what it does.

The sections of a heading

The following is a list of heading sections, but not all sections apply to all programs. Use only those that are useful to your program.

- **Purpose**

  Why was this program written? What does it do?

- **Author**

  It took you a great deal of time and trouble to create this program. Sign your work. Also, when someone else has to modify this program, they can come to you and ask you to explain what you did.

- **Copyright or License**

  Most commercial programs are protected by copyright or trade secret laws. Generally, this is some boilerplate text devised by lawyers. You don't have to understand it, but you should put it in.

- **Warning**

  Sometimes a programmer discovers the hard way that his program contains traps or pitfalls. This section should warn about potential problems. For example: "Don't compile with stack checking on. This is a clever program, and it does strange things with the stack."

- **Usage**

  Briefly explain how to use the program. Oualline's law of documentation states: 90 percent of the time, the documentation is lost. Of the remaining 10 percent, 9 percent of the time the documentation is for a different version of the software and is completely useless. The 1 percent of the time you have the correct documentation, it is written in Chinese.

  A simple way to prevent the program and the documentation from being separated is to put the documentation in the program. You don't need a complete tutorial, just enough for a quick reference.

- **Restrictions**

  This section lists any restrictions that the program might have, such as "This program is designed to process the output of PLOT5 program. It does not do extensive error checking and may behave strangely if given bad input."

- **Algorithms**

  If this program uses any special techniques or algorithms, list them here.

- **References**

  Often a programmer will find it useful to copy or adapt an algorithm from a book or other source (as long as copyright laws are not violated). But give credit where credit is due. Listing the source of any special algorithms in this section gives the people who follow you a chance to check the original work.

- **File Formats**

  This section briefly describes the format of any data files used by the program. This section may also be duplicated in the module that reads or writes the file.

- **Revision History**

  It's not unusual for a number of people to work on a single program over the years. This section lists those who worked on the program, gives a short description of what they did, and tells when the work was done. Revision control software such as RCS and SCCS will automatically generate this information.

- **Note**

  This is a catch-all for any other information you may want future programmers to have.

```
/**********************************************************
 * Analyze - analyze the complexity of a program         *
 *                                                        *
 * Purpose:                                               *
 *      This program produces a set of statistics that    *
 *      are supposed to tell you how complex a program    *
 *      is.                                                *
 *                                                        *
 * Author: John Jones.                                    *
 *                                                        *
```

```
* Copyright 1992 by John Jones.                           *
*                                                         *
* Warning: Compiling with optimization causes             *
*              incorrect code to be generated.            *
*                                                         *
* Restrictions: Works only on error-free C files.         *
*       Does not know about pre-processor directives.     *
*                                                         *
* Algorithm: Uses a classic unbalanced binary tree        *
*       for a symbol table.                               *
*                                                         *
* References: "Software complexity measurements",         *
*       Flying Fingers Newsletter, May 5, 1992            *
*                                                         *
* Output file format for raw data file                    *
*              <magic number>   (ANNUALIZE_MAGIC)         *
*              <# statistics that follow>                 *
*                     <stat table index>                  *
*                     <value>                             *
*                  (Repeat for each statistic)            *
*                                                         *
* Revision history:                                       *
*       1.0 July 5, 1990     Ralph Smith                  *
*                Initial version                          *
*                                                         *
*       1.5 Nov 5, 1990      Bill Green                   *
*                Added comment/code ratio                 *
*                                                         *
*       2.0 Jan 8, 1992      Bill Green                   *
*                Extensive rework of the report generator *
*                                                         *
*       2.1 Jan 30, 1992     Bill Green                   *
*                Ported to MS-DOS                         *
*                                                         *
* Notes: This program generates a lot of numbers          *
*       about your program.  Not all are meaningful.      *
***********************************************************/
```

This particular example is a bit long. It was created to show practical uses of every section. But it illustrates a problem with style guidelines: there is a strong temptation to overdo it. All too often, a programming team will form a style committee, toss around a bunch of ideas for documenting the code, and end up throwing them all into the header. This is almost guaranteed to produce confusing headers that are themselves a maintenance headache.

Heading comments should be as simple as possible, but no simpler.

Too much information is a burden on the programmer. It takes time to type it in and to maintain it. Comments that take a lot of time to create and maintain tempt the programmer to take shortcuts. The result is incorrect or misleading comments, and a *wrong comment is worse than no comment at all*.

Real programs have shorter headers. Here is a header taken from a real program:

```
/*********************************************************
 * lab — handle the labeling of diskettes               *
 *                                                       *
 * Usage:                                                *
 *        lab -w <drive>:<name>   Write label to disk    *
 *        lab -r <drive>:         Read label             *
 *        lab -c <drive>: <drive>: Copy label.           *
 *                                                       *
 *        Copyright 1992 Steve Oualline                  *
 *********************************************************/
#include <stdio.h>
```

Other sections

We've listed a general set of heading sections. You may need additional sections, depending on your environment. For example, a student may be required to put in an assignment number, social security number, and teacher's name. Professional programs may require a part number. Shareware must include a paragraph that asks the user to pay a license fee, along with an address to which users can send money.

Module Headings

Modules are similar to program files, except that there is no main function. Their heading comments are also structured similarly, except that there is no Usage section.

```
/************************************************************
 * symbol.c - Symbol table routines                        *
 *                                                          *
 * Author: Steve Oualline                                   *
 *                                                          *
 * Copyright 1992 Steve Oualline                            *
 *                                                          *
 * Warning: Running out of memory kills the program         *
 *                                                          *
 * Algorithm:                                               *
 *      The symbol table is kept as a balanced binary       *
 *      tree.                                               *
 ************************************************************/
```

Some programmers put a list of the public functions in the heading comments. This is not recommended. First, all the public functions are already listed in the header file for this module. Second, keeping this list up to date requires work, and frequently a programmer will forget to make the updates.

Function Headings

C functions serve much the same purpose as sections of a chapter in a book. They deal with a single subject or operation that the reader can easily absorb.

In this book, each section starts with a section heading in bold letters. This allows the user to scan down a page to locate a section.

A function needs a similar heading. The comment box for a function should contain the following sections:

- **Name**
  The name of the function and a brief comment describing it.

- **Parameters**

  A list of parameters (one per line) and a brief description of each of them. Sometimes the words (returned) or (updated) are added.

- **Return value**

  Describes what value the function returns.

In addition to these standard sections, any other useful information about the function can be added. Here's an example:

```
/***********************************************************
 * find_lowest — find the lowest number in an array       *
 *                                                         *
 * Parameters                                              *
 *      array — the array of integers to search            *
 *      count — number of items in the array               *
 *                                                         *
 * Returns                                                 *
 *      the index of lowest number in the array            *
 *      (in case of a tie, the first instance of the       *
 *      number)                                            *
 ***********************************************************/
int find_lowest(int array[], int count)
```

Some people include another section: Globals Used. This is very useful information, but it is difficult to get and maintain. It takes a lot of work to keep this section current, and frequently a programmer will get lazy and ignore it. It is better not to have a Globals Used section than to have one that is wrong.

Rule 2-6:

Leave out unnecessary comments if they require maintenance and if you are unlikely to maintain them.

When to Write Comments

It is best to put your comments in the program as you are writing it. If you start your program with a set of heading comments, then you should have a pretty good idea what you are planning to do. It helps focus your thoughts.

Avoid the two-step process of coding and later going back and adding comments. This method has several problems. First, you are likely to forget what you did. What may be obvious when you write it may not be so obvious when you re-read it.

Another good reason to write comments while you're writing the code is psychological. When the code is done, you're probably going to feel that the program is done. Adding comments then becomes a chore to be completed as quickly as possible. Generally, this means you'll put in too few comments.

It is especially helpful to do things like screen layouts in comments before you start coding. That way you have a model to work from.

Rule 2-7:

> Comment your code as you write it.

Some Comments on Comments

The heading comments always seem a bit long to the person creating the program. To the person trying to maintain it, they always seem far too short. Balance is the key to good commenting. Make your comments short enough so they aren't bothersome to put in, yet long enough to give other programmers a good idea of what's going on.

Overly commented programs are rare. Usually they turn up in the work of eager first-year programming students.

Under-commented programs are far too frequent. Too many programmers think that their code is obvious. It is not.

There is a reason it is called "code."

Rules

2-1. Keep programs files to no longer than about 2,000 to 3,000 lines.

2-2. Keep all lines in your program files down to 72 characters or fewer.

2-3. Use 8-character tab stops.

2-4. Use only the 95 standard ASCII characters in your programming. Avoid exotic characters.

2-5. Include a heading comment at the beginning of each file that explains the file.

2-6. Leave out unnecessary comments if they require maintenance and if you are unlikely to maintain them.

2-7. Comment your code as you write it.

CHAPTER 3

Variable Names

In English, we put words together to make up sentences. The language is fairly easy to understand when you know what most of the words mean. Even if you don't know some words, you can look them up in the dictionary.

Variables are the "words" for the C language. In a program, variables have a precise definition and usage, but that definition and usage are different for each program. What's worse, some programmers tend to use abbreviations, even for simple things. Shakespeare wrote, "That which we call a rose by any other name would smell as sweet." (*Romeo and Juliet,* Act II, Scene 2). But calling a rose an "RZ" creates needless confusion.

Bureaucratese is a prime example of how things get mixed up when people start using their own unique languages. Government agencies don't fire people, they "dehire" them. That probably wouldn't be confusing to the person being dehired, but consider this example: The Army files "Zipper" under "I." why? Zipper used to be a trade name, making it illegal for Army filing, so they use the generic name "Interlocking cloth fastener." These are the same people who file furry teddy bears under the label "Bears, fur, Edward."

Call a spade a spade. Don't call it "spd", "s1", or "pronged digging implement." Simplicity and a firm grasp of the obvious are necessary for good C programming.

Rule 3-1:
Use simple, descriptive variable names.

A Brief History of the Variable

Early computers were initially used for solving complex and repetitive mathematical equations. Not surprisingly, early programming languages looked a lot like algebra. Mathematicians generally use single-character variable names because they don't *care* what the variables stand for. (They're not supposed to; that's what it means to be a mathematician.)

For example, the equation for the area of a triangle is:

$$a = \tfrac{1}{2}\,bh$$

where *a* is the area of the triangle, *b* is the base, and *h* is the height.

This sort of notation is highly compact. You can express a lot on a single line.

$$\frac{\dfrac{1}{n}\sum U_f U_{f+1} - \left(\dfrac{1}{n}\sum U_f\right)\left(\dfrac{1}{n}\sum U_{f+1}\right)}{\displaystyle\lim_{n\to\infty}\sqrt{\left(\dfrac{1}{n}\sum U_f^{\,2} - \left(\dfrac{1}{n}\sum U_f\right)^2\right)\left(\dfrac{1}{n}\sum U^2{}_{f+k} - \left(\dfrac{1}{n}\sum U_{f+k}\right)^2\right)}}$$

However, it isn't very clear. This simple triangle example requires a somewhat longer line of explanation so we know the meaning of *a*, *b*, and *h*.

In mathematics, you can append notes when you need to break out of the sea of symbols to explain what the symbols stand for. In programming, where code can easily run 10 or more pages and where you care a little more what the symbols stand for, variable names should be more meaningful.

As people discovered that they needed longer variable names, computer languages improved. The first BASIC interpreter limited variables to a single letter and an optional digit (*A, B2, C3*, etc.)

FORTRAN gave the programmer six characters to play with—really 5 1/2, since the first character denoted the default type. That meant that instead of using *I* for an index, you could use a name like *INDEX*. This was progress.

In C the length of a variable name is unlimited (although the first 31 characters must be unique). So variable names like these:

```
disk_name        total_count      last_entry
```

are legal.

If long is better, then very long must be much better, right? Consider this example:

```
total_number_of_entries_with_mangled_or_out_of_range_dates
```

This is an extremely descriptive name; you know exactly what this variable is used for. But there are problems with names like this. First, they are difficult to type. Second, remembering the exact wording of such a long name is not easy. Finally, look at what happens when you try to use this variable in a statement:

```
total_number_of_entries_with_mangled_or_out_of_range_dates =
        total_number_of_entries_with_mangled_input +
        total_number_of_entries_with_mangled_output +
        total_number_of_entries_with_out_of_range_dates;
```

True, you know what the variables are, but the statement logic is obscured by the excess verbosity of the names.

Choosing the right variable name is a balancing act. It must be long enough to be descriptive, yet short enough to be memorable and useful.

Over the years, the following rule of thumb has evolved.

Rule 3-2:

Good variable names are created by using one word or by putting two or three words together, separated by "_". For example:

```
/* Good variable names */
start_time     start_date     late_fee
current_entry  error_count    help_menu
```

Capitalization

Shortly after the invention of moveable type, printers began to arrange their letters in specially designed boxes, or cases. Soon a standard arrangement emerged: two drawers were used for each typeface, the top one holding the capital letters, and the bottom for all the others. Thus the terms upper-case and lower-case.

In many programming languages case is ignored, but in C, upper-case is distinguished from lower-case. This means, for example, that *Count*, *count* and *COUNT* are three different names. This can lead to problems, but it also gives you another tool for making variable names meaningful.

Over the years programmers have devised special naming and capitalization conventions for variables, functions, and constants.

System A:

total_count	Variable and function names	All lower-case words separated by underscores.
NAME_MAX	Constants	All upper-case words separated by underscores.

One of the advantages of this system is that all the component words (total, count, name, max) are separated from each other. This allows you to run the program through a spelling checker.

System B:

TotalCount	Variables and functions	Upper- and lower-case words, not separated.
NAME_MAX	Constants	All upper-case words separated by underscores.

This system uses a different style for variables and functions. Research shows, incidentally, that people find upper- and lower-case words easier to read than lower-case only. System B is not very common.

System C:

total_count	Local variables and functions	All lower-case words separated by underscores.
TotalCount	Global variables and functions	Upper- and lower-case words, not separated.
NAME_MAX	Constants	All upper-case words separated by underscores.

This system uses a different format for local and global names, which provides additional programming information.

Each system has its own advantages. System A used to be the universal standard, but System C is quickly growing in popularity. Choose the one that suits you best and stay with it.

Names You Must Never Use

A programmer once came up with a brilliant way to avoid ever getting a traffic ticket. He submitted a request for a personalized license plate with the choices "O0O0O0", "lllll1", and "l1O0ll". He figured that if his license plate read "O0O0O0", the police would find it difficult to tell the difference between the letter "O" and the digit "0". The problem was, the DMV clerk had the same problem, so he got a personalized license plate that read "OOOOOO".

The upper-case letter "O" and the digit "0" can easily be confused. So can the lower-case letter "l" and the digit "1".

Rule 3-3:

Never use *l* (lower-case L) or *O* (upper-case O) as variable or constant names.

Other Names Not To Use

Don't use names already in the C library. You'll never know who calls them. I recently ported a program that defined its own version of *getdate*. The program worked under UNIX because although the C library has a *getdate* function, the program never expected to use it.

When the application was ported to the PC, I discovered that *getdate* called the library function time. This function had an internal call to *getdate*. It expected to call the system *getdate*, not a local function defined in the program. But the program overrode the library's *getdate*, which resulted in *getdate* calling *time* calling *getdate* calling *time*—until the stack overflowed.

A quick global rename was done to turn *getdate* into *get_current_date*, and the porting problem went away. But it would have never occurred in the first place if the programmer hadn't used an existing C library function:

Rule 3-4:

Don't use the names of existing C library functions or constants.

Avoid Similar Names

Subtle differences in variable names should be avoided. For example, the variable names *total* and *totals* can be easily confused. Differences between variables should be blatant, such as *entry_total* and *all_total*.

Rule 3-5:

Don't use variable names that differ by only one or two characters. Make every name obviously different from every other name.

Consistency in Naming

Consistency and repetition are extremely powerful programming tools. Use similar names for similar functions. In the following example, you can easily guess the name of the missing variable:

```
int start_hour;      /* Hour when the program began */
int start_minute;    /* Minute when the program began */
int ??????          /* Second when the program began */
```

If *start_hour* is the hour when the program began and *start_minute* is the minute, you can easily figure out the name of the variable that holds the seconds. Think how confusing it would be if the programmer had written this:

```
int start_hour;      /* Hour when the program began */
int begin_minute;    /* Program start time, minutes only */

/* Seconds on the clock at program commencement */
int commence_seconds;
```

Rule 3-6:

> Use similar names for variables that perform similar functions.

Which Word First

Suppose you have a variable that denotes the maximum entry in a series of numbers. You could call it *max_entry* or *entry_max*. How do you decide which name to use?

Picking one at random is does not work, because you might at one time pick *max_entry* for one program and *entry_max* for another. Experience shows that too often we forget which one we picked for a particular program, which results in confusion. More often than I care to mention, I've had to do a global search and replace to change *max_entry* to *entry_max*.

You need a selection rule. What happens when you put the most important word first (in this case, *entry*)? A cross reference listing will group all the entry-related variables together, such as (*entry_count, entry_min, entry_max*).

If you choose to begin with the word max, then all the maximum limits will be grouped together (*max_count, max_entry, max_list*).

Sorting by an important relation (all variables related to entries) is more important than sorting by type (all maximums).

Rule 3-7:

> When creating a two-word variable name where the words can be put in any order, always put the more important word first.

Standard Prefixes and Suffixes

Over the years a few standard prefixes and suffixes have developed for variable names. These include the following:

_ptr   Suffix for pointer

Examples:
```
int *entry_ptr; /* Pointer to current entry */
char *last_ptr; /* Pointer to last char in str */
```

_p   Another suffix for pointer. This can be a little confusing to people who are not familiar with it, so the suffix *_ptr* is preferred.

Examples:
```
event *next_p;/* Pointer to next event in queue */
char *word_p; /* Pointer to start of next word */
```

_file a   Variable of type FILE *.

Examples:
```
FILE *in_file;      /* Input data file */
FILE *database_file;/*Where we put the database */
```

_fd   File descriptor (returned by the *open* function.)

Examples:
```
/* The dictionary file descriptor */
int dictionary_fd;

/* File where we put the memory dump */
int dump_fd;
```

*n_*   Number of. For example, if you store a set of events in the array events, the *n_events* is the number of entries in the events array. Does this violate the rule about putting the most important word first? Yes, but it's established usage.

Examples:
```
/* A list of events */
```

```
int events[EVENT_MAX];

/* Number of items in event array */
int n_events = 0;

/* A list of accounts */
struct account account;

/* Number of accounts seen so far */
int n_accounts = 0;
```

Rule 3-8:

Standard prefixes and suffixes are *_ptr, _p, _file, _fd,* and *n_*.

Module Prefixes

When creating large modules or libraries (more than 10 functions), a prefix is sometimes added to each variable and function in the library. For example, everything in a database library might start with the prefix *Db*.

Example:
```
int DbErrorNumber;
extern int DbOpen(char *name);
extern int DbClose(int handle);
```

This serves two purposes: first, it identifies the module containing the name; and second, it limits name conflicts. A symbol table module and a database both might have a lookup function, but the names *SymLookup* and *DbLookup* do not conflict.

The X Windows system uses this naming convention extensively. All X Windows functions begin with the letter X. However, the system is so complex that it has been further divided into "tool kits," each of which has its own prefix. For example, *Xt* is the Andrew Tool kit, *Xv* is the X-view tool kit, etc.

Special Prefixes and Suffixes

Sometimes you need to use special names, names that you can be sure don't conflict with a large body of existing code. Such cases call for unusual naming conventions.

For example, the C preprocessor had been around a number of years before the ANSI Committee decided on a standard set of predefined symbols. In order to avoid conflict, they decided that each symbol would look like this: *(_ _ SYMBOL _ _)*.

Some of the predefined symbols include:

```
_ _LINE_ _           _ _FILE_ _           _ _STDC_ _
```

Compiler manufacturers have now jumped on this bandwagon and defined their own special symbols using this convention.

The utilities *lex* and *yacc* solve the naming problem in a different way: they begin everything with yy. Thus we get names like *yylex*, *yytext*, and *yylength* in the code generated by these utilities. It may look a little strange at first, but after a yywhile yyou yyget yyused to it.

If you do need to define a name that's widely used and you want to minimize the possibility of a naming conflict, begin it with an underscore (_). Very few programmers use this character at the beginning of normal variable or constant names.

When You Can Use Short Names

In some cases you can use short variable names. For example, when dealing with a graphic position, the variables *x* and *y* are descriptive.

Also, the variable *i* is frequently used as a general-purpose, handy dandy, local index. Its popularity makes it acceptable as a variable name, even though the name *index* is more descriptive.

Rule 3-9:

> Short names such as *x*, *y*, and *i* are acceptable when their meaning is clear and when a longer name would not add information or clarity.

argv, argc

The *main* function of a C program takes two arguments. In 99 percent of the programs, the arguments are named argv and argc. In the other 1 percent, we wish the programmer had used *argc* and *argv* instead of *ac* and *av*.

A lot of history has gone into these names. When programmers see them, they immediately think "command line arguments." Don't confuse the issue by using these names for anything else.

Rule 3-10:

> Use *argc* for the number of command line arguments and *argv* for the argument list. Do not use these names for anything else.

Microsoft Notation

When Microsoft introduced Windows, it also introduced a new variable-naming notation called Hungarian Notation. (There are two reasons why it's called that. First, Charles Simonyi, the man who invented it, is Hungarian. Second, most people looking at it for the first time think that it might as well be written in Hungarian.) It's also known as Microsoft Notation.

The idea is simple: prefix each variable name with a letter denoting its type; for example, *w* for a 16-byte integer (word), and *l* for a 32-byte integer (long). That way, you can easily prevent programming problems caused by type conflicts. For example:

```
wValue = lParam;        /* Obvious type conflict */
```

There is no complete list of prefixes. The following was gathered from several sources:

Prefix	Type
b	Boolean (true or false)
w	Word, 16-bit integer
i	Integer, 16-bit integer (conflicts with *w*)
n	Short, 16-bit integer (conflicts with *w*)
n	Near pointer (ambiguous, can be used for "short")
p	Pointer
d	Double, 32-bit integer
dw	Double word, 32-bit integer (conflicts with *d*)
l	Long, 32-bit integer (conflicts with *d*)
fn	Function (or pointer to function)
g	Global
s	String
sz	String terminated with zero (conflicts with *s*)
c	character

by	byte (unsigned character)
h	Window handle
hn	Window handle (conflicts with *h*)

There are some problems with this notation. First, the list of prefixes is confusing and incomplete, and the order of prefixes is not clear. For example, does a pointer to a word start with *pw* or *wp*?

Second, variables with type prefixes get sorted by type in the cross reference, which is not the most useful ordering.

Of course, sometimes a programmer really needs to put type information into a variable name. For example, it's very important to know the difference between things and pointers to things. The suffix *_ptr* does this job well.

Example:
```
char name[30];   /* Name of the user */
char *name_ptr; /* Pointer to user's name */
```

Suffixes easily do the job of Microsoft's prefixes without getting in the way. The only advantage of Microsoft Notation is that it makes type conflicts obvious. For example:

```
wValue = lParam;        /* Obvious type conflict */
```

However, most good compilers will produce a warning message for potential problems like this. So while it may be hard to spot the potential problem in the following line:

```
count = index;
```

it's a lot easier when the compiler chimes in with:

```
Line 86:  Warning: Assignment may lose significant digits
```

Imaginative Solutions

PC-class machines come with a line-drawing character set that allows the programmer to construct things like single-and double-lined boxes. One of the problems PC programmers face is what to name these curious characters when they are referred to in a program. One solution is to begin every single line character with S, followed by the character type: C for corner, L for line, T for T and X for cross, followed by a name. The result is:

Character	Name
┐	*S_C_UR* (Single, Corner, Upper Right)
┌	*S_C_UL* (Single, Corner, Upper Left)
┘	*S_C_LR* (Single, Corner, Lower Right)
└	*S_C_LL* (Single, Corner, Lower Left)
–	*S_L_A* (Single, Line, Across)
│	*S_C_UR* (Single, Line Down)
+	*SD_X_DA* (Single Down, crossing Double Across)

After a while this system tends to make you sick. The problem with this system is that it's complex and somewhat error-prone. At the time it was the best we could come up with, but that didn't stop us from trying something new.

Then someone figured out a system where you started at the top and worked your way around, counting the number of lines (0, 1, or 2).

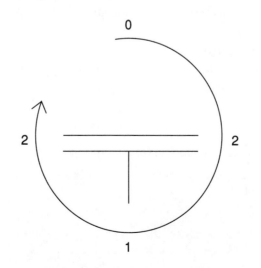

So the character turns into L_0212. The table is now:

Character	Name
⌐	*L_0011*
⌐	*L_0110*
⌐	*L_1001*
∟	*L_1100*
–	*L_0101*
		L_1010
+	*L_1212*

Now, these names break all the rules we have discussed so far. They are short and somewhat cryptic. But put them in a file with a very good comment block explaining them, and they bring order to a very messy problem.

Case studies

Over the years different groups have developed their own standard naming conventions. Each has its own advantages and disadvantages. This section will look at some of the standard programs and how they use their names.

The C runtime library

The C runtime library traces its roots back to the first C compiler. It evolved over the years, and the ANSI Committee standardized it.

Naming conventions:

Private variable names	All lower-case
Public variable names	All lower-case
Constant names	Upper-case only

The C library is full of short, cryptic names like these:

```
creat   stdin   stdout  open
strcpy  printf  memcmp  malloc
```

Initially names were restricted because of severe limitations in the compiler, which ran on some extremely small machines. Also, the early programmers didn't place any value on long names.

These names are somewhat cryptic. For example, the function strcpy copies a string. A much better name would have been *string_copy*. And using *creat* instead of *create* is pretty silly.

The language does not make good use of prefix and suffix letters. For example, here is the *printf* family of functions:

printf	Print to standard output
fprintf	Print to a file
sprintf	Print to a string
vfprintf	Print to a file, argument list is a vector

Also, the library is fairly consistent. For example, every string function *str...* has a corresponding *strn...* function.

Example:

strcpy	copy a string
strncpy	copy n characters of a string
strcat	append one string to another
strncat	append n characters of one string to another

Constant names are also somewhat cryptic. For example, some of the error codes (from standard library *errno.h*) are:

```
#define EZERO    0    /* Error 0                      */
#define EINVFNC  1    /* Invalid function number  */
#define ENOFILE  2    /* File not found              */
#define ENOPATH  3    /* Path not found              */
#define ECONTR   7    /* Memory blocks destroyed  */
#define EINVMEM  9    /* Invalid memory block address */
```

However, the C library is good about grouping similar constants together. All error numbers begin with *E*, all open flags begin *O_*, and so on.

All in all, the C library is fairly well designed; and the naming, though short, is regular and reasonable, with limitations traceable to the days when C compilers were much more limited.

The UNIX kernel

The UNIX operating system was one of the very first to be written in a high-level language. It was the first to be widely ported. Today, almost every computer that's not a PC clone runs UNIX.

Naming conventions:

Private variable names	All lower-case
Public variable names	All lower-case
Constant names	Upper-case only

UNIX is the king of the 1- to 3-character variable names. Some typical names are:

```
u       bp      i       bn
pid     uid     gid     fd
```

After a while, UNIX operating system programmers learn the meaning of most of the abbreviations. They know that *pid* stands for process *id* and *bp* is a buffer pointer. But it takes time and effort to learn this code. In fact, UNIX internal programming is not for the inexperienced or the faint of heart. Most programmers must be introduced into the world of UNIX internals by an experienced guru.

As UNIX evolved, more and more people added to its code. While the core of the system remains cryptic, much of the new code is better. Longer variable names came into use, such as:

```
physical_io     dispatch
signal          tty_select
```

This helps, but at heart UNIX is a difficult beast to like. The UNIX internals are a good example of what not to do.

The Microsoft Windows library

Microsoft Windows provides PC programmers with a graphics programming environment. It also allows programmers to better use the power of the more advanced 80386 and 80486 processors.

Naming conventions:

Private variable names   Up to the application programmer

Public variable names   Upper- and lower-case

Constant names   Upper-case only

Function names in Microsoft Windows are nicely done, consisting of several words put together. Examples:

```
GetFreeSpace    UnlockSegment   CreateBitmap
CloseClipboard  GetWindow       AppendMenu
```

However, there is no special prefix or suffix for Windows functions, so it's impossible to tell at a glance whether or not *OpenFile* is a Windows function. Constants are all upper-case.

Examples:

```
LB_SETSEL    WM_MOUSE    WM_MOVE
WM_CLOSE     EN_UPDATE   LB_MSGMAX
```

Each constant contains a short group prefix. For example, all "List box"-related constants begin with *LB_*. Almost all Windows constants contain only one "_", which is used to separated the prefix from the rest of the constant. Multiple words are run together, making it difficult to read. Therefore a constant like *WM_WINDOWPOSCHANGED* would be much more readable if it was written as *WM_WINDOW_POS_CHANGED*.

In general, the Windows naming convention makes programs more readable than the UNIX code or C library. Although not perfect, it is a step forward.

X Windows

X Windows is a popular UNIX windowing system available from MIT. Its low cost and relative availability make it the windowing system of choice for most UNIX systems.

Naming conventions:

Private variable names	Up to the application programmer
Public variable names	Upper- and lower-case
Constant names	Most upper-case only, some upper- and lower-case

One of the most refreshing things about X Windows programming is that it actually looks like someone thought about the design and style of the system before beginning the coding.

Public function and variable names in X Windows are upper- and lower-case words, with no underscores.

Examples:

```
XDrawString        XNextEvent         XGrabPointer
XCreateGC          XMapWindow         XFlush
```

All public names start with the letter X. The programmer can select among many different tool kits for code. Each of these has its own prefix. For example, all routines in the X-View tool kit start with *Xv*.

Constants begin with a type prefix. For example, all button-related constants begin with *BUTTON_*. Constants are a series of words separated by underscores.

```
XA_POINT           XA_BITMAP          XA_ATOM
XrmOptionNoArg     XSetSizeHints      FocusIn
```

The X Windows system shows what can happen when some thought is given to style before coding begins. It is well-designed and presents the programmer with one of the best interfaces available.

Variable Declaration Comments

Choosing good variable names helps create programs that are easy to read and maintain. But names can't do the job alone. The programmer needs a definition for each variable. Technical books have glossaries that explain all the special terms. We also need a glossary for our programs.

Writing a glossary is a lot of work. Maintaining it and keeping it up to date is even more work. A better solution is to follow each variable with a comment that describes it.

Examples:
```
int  window;          /* Current window index */
int  words;           /* Number of words in the document */
int  line_number;     /* Current input file line number */
char *in_name;        /* Current input file name */
```

Now, if you want to know the definition of *line_number*, go to your cross reference and look for the first reference to the variable, thus locating the line:

```
int  line_number;        /* Current input file line number */
```

Using this method, you can quickly determine the type and definition of any variable.

Rule 3-11:

Follow every variable declaration with a comment that defines it.

Units

Weather services generally measure rainfall in hundredths of inches, referring to half an inch of rain as 50. However, one night the weather service computer used inches as input. Someone forgot a decimal point and entered 50 instead of 0.50.

Now, 50 inches of rain is a lot of rain. The computer caught the error and printed this message:

```
Build an Ark. Gather the animals two by two.
```

Units of measure are important. It's one thing to describe *dist* as the distance between two objects, but what are the units? They could be inches, centimeters, yards, meters, or light years. It makes a difference.

Rule 3-12:

Whenever possible, include the units of measure in the description of a variable.

Examples:
```
int distance_left;  /* Distance we've got left (in miles) */
int owed;     /* Amount owed in current account (in cents) */


/* Acceleration of gravity (in furlongs/fortnight**2) */
float gravity;
```

I once had to write a graphics conversion program. Many different units were used throughout the system, including inches, thousandths of an inch, plotter units, digitizer units, etc. Figuring out which units to use was a nightmare. Finally, I gave up and put the following comment in the program:

```
/**********************************************************
 * Warning:  I have no idea what the input units to     *
 * this program are, nor do I have any idea what output *
 * units are used, but I do know that if you divide by  *
 * 3 the plots look about the right size.               *
 **********************************************************/
```

Structures and unions

A structure is simply a group of related variables tied together to form a convenient package. Each field in a structure should be treated like a variable, with a carefully chosen name. A descriptive comment is necessary as well.

Example:
```
/*
 * A square of space on the screen enclosed by
 * a border
 */
struct box {
    int x;      /* X loc. of upper left corner (in pixels) */
    int y;      /* Y loc. of upper left corner (in pixels) */
    int length; /* Length of the box in pixels */
    int width;  /* Width of the box in pixels */
};
```

The structure itself is described in a comment just before its definition. This example uses a multi-line comment to describe the box. Single-line comments tend to get lost in the clutter. White space before and after the definition separates the structure from the rest of the code (much like blank lines separate paragraphs in this book).

Rule 3-13:

> Name and comment each field in a structure or union like a variable.

Rule 3-14:

> Begin each structure or union definition with a multi-line comment describing it.

Rule 3-15:

> Put at least one blank line before and after a structure or union definition.

Long declarations and comments

Sometimes a variable declaration and its initializer leave little room for a comment. In the following example, we need to describe *last_entry*, but where do we put the comment?

```
int first_entry;        /* First entry to process */
int last_entry = (GOOD_ENTRIES + BAD_ENTRIES + FUDGE);
```

```
int current_entry;      /* Entry we are working on */
```

There's no room at the end of the line. The solution is to put the description on a separate line in front of the variable:

```
int first_entry;        /* First entry to process */
/* Last entry number to process */
int last_entry = (GOOD_ENTRIES + BAD_ENTRIES + FUDGE);
int current_entry;      /* Entry we are working on */
```

But this is still not good enough. This section of code looks like a big gray blob. It's not easy to locate the description for *last_entry*. Adding white space not only breaks up the blob, it also helps group *last_entry*'s comment and declaration as shown here:

```
int first_entry;        /* First entry to process */

/* Last entry number to process */
int last_entry = (GOOD_ENTRIES + BAD_ENTRIES + FUDGE);

int current_entry;      /* Entry we are working on */
```

Rule 3-16:

When you can't put a descriptive comment at the end of a variable declaration, put it on a separate line above. Use blank lines to separate the declaration/comment pair from the rest of the code.

Group similar declarations

Repetition and consistency are powerful organizing tools. When declaring variables, group similar variables together and use similar names.

```
int errors_out;   /* Total number of output errors */
int errors_in;    /* Total number of input errors */
```

```
int max_out;        /* Max output error rate (errors/hour) */
int max_in;         /* Max input error rate (errors/hour) */

int min_out;        /* Min output error rate (errors/hour) */
int min_in;         /* Min input error rate (errors/hour) */
```

This example uses the prefix *errors_* for the counters that accumulate a running total of the input/output errors. The variables that hold the limits start with the prefixes *max_* and *min_*. Common suffixes are also used. All output-related variables end with *_out*, and input variables with *_in*.

Notice that each group of variables consists of two declarations, the first one for the output and the second one for the input.

This example shows only one of several possible groupings. Another possible method is this:

```
int errors_out;     /* Total number of output errors */
int max_out;        /* Max output error rate (errors/hour) */
int min_out;        /* Min output error rate (errors/hour) */

int errors_in;      /* Total number of input errors */
int max_in;         /* Max input error rate (errors/hour) */
int min_in;         /* Min input error rate (errors/hour) */
```

Rule 3-17:

Group similar variables together. When possible, use the same structure for each group.

Hidden Variables

Hidden variables occur when a variable is declared in a global scope and is then declared again in a local scope. The second declaration "hides" the first.

In the following example, the second declaration of location hides the first.

```
/* Bad programming practice */

/* Distance traveled by the car in miles */

float location;

/* . . . */
void display_location(void)
{
    /* Location of current cursor */
    int location;   /* *** Hides previous declaration *** */
```

The problem is that we've now used the same word for two different things. Is location a global or a local? Is it a **float** or an **int**? Without knowing which version of the variable is being referred to, we can't answer these questions.

There are enough variable names in the universe that there's no reason to use the same name twice. We could just as easily have used a different name for the second declaration:

```
/* Good programming practice */

/* Distance traveled by the car in miles */
float location;

/* . . . */
void display_location(void)
{
    /* Location of current cursor */
    int cursor_location;
```

Rule 3-18:
Don't use hidden variables.

Portable Types

The C compiler runs on many different machines. Making portable programs that can run on all these machines is an art. One trick used to define portable types. For example, Novell uses the type *WORD* and *DWORD* in all its header files. But what is a *WORD*? Is it 8, 16, or 32 bits? Is it signed or unsigned? You can't tell from the name.

A better set of portable names is:

```
INT16  INT32
UINT16 UINT32
```

These names clearly define the type and size of the data.

Rule 3-19:

> Use the names *INT16*, *INT32*, *UINT16*, and *UINT32* for portable applications.

Numbers

C uses a wide variety of numbers, and it's easy to get them confused. Be careful to make numbers clear and unambiguous.

Floating-point numbers

Here are some examples of floating-point numbers:

```
0.5        .3        6.2       10.
32E4       1e+10     0.333331  5E-5
```

A zero in front of the decimal point is optional. For example, C treats 0.8 and .8 the same. But there is a difference. .8 looks a lot like the integer 8, while the number 0.8 is obviously floating-point. Similarly, you should write numbers like 5. as 5.0.

Rule 3-20:

> Floating-point numbers must have at least one digit on either side of the decimal point.

Large floating-point numbers are written using exponent format. The exponent's "E" can be written in upper- or lower-case. Which is better? Well, all digits are full-height characters. The upper-case E is also a full-height character and can easily get lost in a string of digits:

```
321418312354321E132809932
```

The E is important and shouldn't get lost. The lower-case is easier to spot:

```
321418312354321e132809932
```

It's even easier if you always include the sign.

```
321418312354321e+132809932
```

So a lower-case e and a sign make these important elements of a floating-point number stand out.

Rule 3-21:

> The exponent in a floating-point number must be a lower-case *e*. This is always followed by a sign.

Here are some examples of good floating-point numbers:

```
3.1415        3.0          0.5          0.0
1.0e+33       1.0e-333.    33.0         1230.0
```

Hex numbers

C uses the prefix *0x* for hexadecimal numbers. A upper- or lower-case *x* may be used, but as discussed, lower-case letters stand out better.

Rule 3-22:

> Start hexadecimal numbers with *0x*. (Lower-case *x* only.)

Hexadecimal digits include the letters A through F. Again, upper- or lower-case may be used, so *0xACE* is the same as *0Xace*. Lower-case digits create numbers that are easily confused with variable names. Upper-case digits create numbers that look like constants.

```
0xace       ace        face      0Xdead
0xACE       X_ACE      BEEF      0xBEEF
```

Numbers are a type of constant, so confusing a number and a constant is not too problematic. Mistaking a number for a variable is worse, so it is preferable to use upper-case digits.

Rule 3-23:

Use upper-case *A* through *F* when constructing hexadecimal constants.

Long integers

Long integers end with the letter L. Again, C is case insensitive, so lower-case l can be used. But lower-case l looks a lot like the number 1 and should be avoided. For example, the following two constants look very much alike:

```
341         341
```

But when the long integer is written using an upper-case L, the confusion clears up:

```
34L         341
```

Rule 3-24:

Long constants should end with an upper-case *L*.

Rules

3-1. Use simple, descriptive variable names.

3-2. Good variable names can be created by using one word or by putting two or three words together, separated by an underscore (_).

3-3. Never use *l* (lower-case L) or *O* (upper-case O) as variable or constant names.

3-4. Don't use the names of existing C library functions or constants.

3-5. Don't use variable names that differ by only one or two characters. Variable names should be obviously different.

3-6. Use similar names for variables that perform similar functions.

3-7. When creating a two-word variable name where the words can be put in any order, always put the most important word first.

3-8. Standard prefixes and suffixes are _ptr_, _p_, _file_, _fd_, and _n_.

3-9. Short names such as _x_, _y_, and _i_ are acceptable when their meaning is clear and when a longer name would not add information or clarity.

3-10. Use _argc_ for the number of command line arguments and _argv_ for the argument list. Do not use these names for anything else.

3-11. Follow every variable declaration with a comment that defines it.

3-12. Whenever possible, include the units of measure in the description of a variable.

3-13. Name and comment each field in a structure or union like a variable.

3-14. Begin each structure or union definition with a multi-line comment that defines it.

3-15. Put at least one blank line before and after a structure or union definition.

3-16. When you can't put a descriptive comment at the end of a variable declaration, put it on a separate line above. Use blank lines to separate the declaration/comment pair from the rest of the code.

3-17. Group similar variables together. When possible, use the same structure for each group.

3-18. Don't use hidden variables.

3-19. Use the names _INT16_, _INT32_, _UINT16_, and _UINT32_ for portable applications.

3-20. Floating-point numbers must have at least one digit on either side of the decimal point.

3-21. The exponent in a floating-point number must be a lower-case e. This is always followed by a sign.

3-22. Start hexadecimal number with _0x_. (Lower-case _x_ only.)

3-23. Use upper-case _A_ through _F_ when constructing hexadecimal constants.

3-24. Long constants should end with an upper-case _L_.

## CHAPTER 4

Statement Formatting

Organization is the key to a well-written program. Good programming style helps present the detail and logic of your program in a clear and easy-to-understand manner.

Programming style and aesthetics are related. A well-written program is pleasing to look at, read, and understand. Your goal in formatting a program is to make it look neat, well-organized, and beautiful.

Formatting the Body of the Program

The sentence is a basic unit of writing. A sentence ends with a terminator: a question mark, exclamation point, or period. In C, the basic coding unit is the statement. C statements do not have terminators, like sentences; rather, they are separated from each other by semicolons (;).

Well laid-out programs allow the programmer to quickly and easily pick out the statement within the program. Running the code together, as shown in the following example, hurts readability and clarity:

```
/* Poor programming practice */
biggest=-1;first=0;count=57;init_key_words();
if(debug)open_log_files();table_size=parse_size+lex_size;
```

How many statements are in this program fragment? It's hard to tell. The programmer has tried to compact the program by putting as much on each line as possible. It's much like the old limerick:

> *There was a young man from Iran*
> *Whose verses just would not quite scan.*
> *When someone asked why,*
> *He gave this reply:*
> *"I like to put as many words on the last line as I possibly can."*

It's easier to pick out the statements when there is only one statement per line:

```
/* Better programming practice (still needs work) */
biggest=-1;
first=0;
count=57;
init_key_words();
if(debug)
    open_log_files();
table_size=parse_size+lex_size;
```

Rule 4-1:

Write one statement per line.

There are still some problems with this fragment. True, it is much easier to find the statements, but they are still hard to read. The problem is that our eyes are trained to treat a set of letters and symbols as one word. Writinga-sentencewithnospacesmakesitveryhardtoread. Similarly writing a C statement with no spaces makes it hard to read.

Rule 4-2:

Put spaces before and after each arithmetic operator, just like you put spaces between words when you write.

```
/* Still better, but not quite there */
biggest = -1;
first = 0;
count = 57;
init_key_words();
if(debug)
```

```
    open_log_files();
table_size = parse_size + lex_size;
```

Adding spaces not only improves readability, it also helps to eliminate errors. Consider the statement:

```
*average = *total / *count;    /* Compute the average */
```

Written without spaces this becomes:

```
*average=*total/*count;        /* Compute the average */
```

Looks like the same statement, but it's not. Can you spot the problem?

The operators slash (/) and star (*) take on a new meaning when they are put together with no space. The operator /* is the beginning of a comment. So the result of the compression is:

```
*average=*total    /* count;  /* Compute the average */
```

If you have a good C compiler, you will get a warning about nested comments. If you have a typical compiler, you'll get nothing.

Now back to our program fragment. Spaces makes the individual statements easier to read, but the entire fragment is still something of a gray blob. We can do better.

This book is broken up into paragraphs. The paragraph markers separate one set of sentences from another. In C, you can use blank lines to separate code into paragraphs:

```
/* Finally something decent */
biggest = -1;
first = 0;
count = 57;

init_key_words();

if (debug)
    open_log_files();
table_size = parse_size + lex_size;
```

The result is a section of code that uses space to separate the coding elements into pleasantly arranged groups.

Simplifying complex statements

Sometimes a statement such as an assignment statement grows so long and complex that it can't fit on one line. In such cases, consider turning a big complex statement into several smaller, simpler statements.

For example, this is syntactically correct, but messy:

```
/* This is a big mess */
gain = (old_value - new_value) /
       (total_old - total_new) * 100.0;
```

It can be rewritten as three smaller statements:

```
/* Good practice */
delta_value = (old_value - new_value);
delta_total = (total_old - total_new);
gain = delta_value / delta_total * 100.0;
```

Rule 4-3:

Change a long, complex statement into several smaller, simpler statements.

Splitting long statements

An alternative to turning one statement into two is to split long statements into multiple lines.

Splitting is an art. The idea is to split the line in a way that does not add confusion. There is a rule: One statement per line. A two-line statement breaks that rule, so always indent the second line to indicate that it is a continuation.

Rule 4-4:

In a statement that consists of two or more lines, every line except the first must be indented an extra level to indicate that it is a continuation of the first line.

For example:

```
net_profit = gross_profit - overhead -
             cost_of_goods - payroll;
```

This example brings up another question: Do you put operators at the end of the line, as in the previous example, or at the beginning of the next line?

```
net_profit = gross_profit - overhead
             - cost_of_goods - payroll;
```

Actually, either method is acceptable as long as it is used consistently. That means that I don't get to dodge the issue if there is any reasonable basis for choosing one method over the other.

There is a basis: majority rule. Most programmers prefer to put the operators at the end of the line. So let's go with the majority preference and make it the rule:

Rule 4-5:
> When writing multi-line statements, put the arithmetic and logical operators at the end of each line.

Splitting and parentheses. Complex statements in C can contain several levels of parentheses. The following example shows a complex statement that contains many parentheses. The comment below it indicates the nesting level.

```
result = (((x1 + 1) * (x1 + 1)) - ((y1 + 1) * (y1 + 1)));
/* nest   1233333333222233333333211123333333322223333333321 */
```

The best place to break the line is where the nesting level is lowest; in this case at the - operator in the middle:

```
result = (((x1 + 1) * (x1 + 1)) -
          ((y1 + 1) * (y1 + 1)));
```

Rule 4-6:

When breaking up a line, the preferred split point is where the parenthetic nesting is lowest.

The second line of the example is carefully indented so that the parenthesis line up. Why not align it with the first parenthesis?

```
/* Don't program like this */
result = (((x1 + 1) * (x1 + 1)) -
         ((y1 + 1) * (y1 + 1)));
```

Notice that the lines seem to be a little off. That's because the first line's Level 1 parenthesis is in the same column as the second line's Level 2 parenthesis.

```
/* Don't Program like this */
```
$$result = (_1(_2(_3x1 + 1)_3 * (_3x1 + 1)_3)_2 -$$
$$(_2(_3y1 + 1)_3 * (_3y1 + 1)_3)_2)_1;$$

Properly aligned (Level 2 to Level 2), the same statement looks like this:

$$result = (_1(_2(_3x1 + 1)_3 * (_3x1 + 1)_3)_2 -$$
$$(_2(_3y1 + 1)_3 * (_3y1 + 1)_3)_2)_1;$$

Rule 4-7:

Align like level parentheses vertically.

Here's a more complex example:

```
flag = (result == OK) ||
       ((result == WARNING) &&
       ((code == WARN_SHORT) ||
        (code == WARN_EOF))
       );
```

The indentation in this example gives the programmer several clues about the statement's logic. First, there are two major clauses:

```
(result == OK) ||
```

and

```
((result == WARNING) &&
 ((code == WARN_SHORT) ||
  (code == WARN_EOF))
);
```

They are indented at the same level. The second clause goes on for four lines. This is obvious because its beginning and ending parenthesis have the same indent. The two (*code* == lines carry equal weight and are at the same level. Their beginning parenthesis are aligned in the same column.

As you can see, proper splitting and indentation of a multi-line statement can provide a great deal of information about the logic and structure of the program.

Splitting a for statement. A **for** statement is unique, since it is three statements in one. The general format of a **for** is this:

```
for (<initialization>; <condition>; <increment>)
```

The *<initialization>*, *<condition>*, and *<increment>* are three complete C statements. If these statements have any complexity at all, the entire **for** statement is likely to overflow the line. Whenever a **for** grows too long for one line, split it first at the component statement boundaries.

For example, this line:

```
for (index = start; data[index] != 0; index++)
```

splits like this:

```
for (index = start;
     data[index] != 0;
     index++)
```

Note that we've aligned the beginnings of the three substatements.

Rule 4-8:

Split long **for** statements along statement boundaries.

In the previous example, we turned a one-line **for** statement into three. But if the statement is short enough, can you limit it to two lines?

```
/* Poor practice */
for (index = start; data[index] != 0;
     index++)
```

The answer is no. The problem is that this split is ambiguous. We could just as easily have written this:

```
/* Poor practice */
for (index = start;
     data[index] != 0; index++)
```

Consistency is part of good style. If you do things consistently, you set up expectations, which is another way of saying you remove one detail that the reader of the program has to figure out. Don't split a **for** statement one way one time and another the next. You can consistently split a **for** statement into three lines the same way every time, but there is no preferred two-line split. Two-line splits introduce inconsistency. Avoid them.

Rule 4-9:

Always split a **for** statement into three lines.

Splitting a switch statement. The **switch** statement is the most complex statement in the C language. The rule for splitting it is very simple: Don't. If the index expression for a **switch** statement grows too big for one line, split it into two different statements: an assignment and a **switch**.

For example:

```
/* Bad practice */
    switch (state_list[cur_state].next_state +
            goto_list[last_last] +
            special_overrides)  {
```

should be turned into:

```
/* Good practice */
    switch_index =  (state_list[cur_state].next_state +
                     goto_list[last_last] +
                     special_overrides);
    switch (switch_index) {
```

Rule 4-10:
>   Write **switch** statements on a single line.

Conditional operators (? :). When splitting an expression containing a conditional operation (? :), try to put the entire conditional clause on a line by itself.

```
/* Good practice (preferred) */
    result = past_due +
        (total_owed > 0) ? total_owed : 0;
```

Rule 4-11:
>   Keep conditionals on a single line if possible.

If the conditional clause itself is too long for one line, it can be split into three lines. The format is this:

```
(condition) ?
    (true-value) :
    (false-value)
```

Each line contains one component of the expression. Since the true-value and false-value are sub-sections of the conditional, their lines are indented.

Rule 4-12:

When splitting a conditional clause (? :), write it on three lines: the condition line, the true-value line, and the false-value line. Indent the second and third line an extra level.

Side effects

When writing a children's story, you must keep the sentence structure simple and avoid compound sentences. Well, a computer is not a child; it doesn't have that much intelligence. But in C coding, you should do anything you can to simply the program. That means avoiding side effects.

A side effect is an operation that is performed in addition the main operation of a statement. For example, the statement:

```
current = count[index++]
```

assigns current a value and increments index. Look out. Any time you start using "and" to describe what a statement does, you're in trouble. The same statement could just as easily have been written this way:

```
current = count[index]
index++;
```

This way, there are no side effects.

C allows very free use of the ++ and -- operators within other statements. Taking advantage of this freedom can create all sorts of problems. Consider the statement:

```
i = 0;
out[i++] = in[i++];
```

In fact, consider it a test. Exactly what does this program do?

A) Evaluate out*[i]* as out*[0]*, increment *i* (*i* is now 1), evaluate *in[i]* as in*[1]*, increment i (i is now 2), do the assignment (*out[0]* = *in[i]*).

B) Evaluate *in[i]* as in*[0]*, increment *i* (*i* is now 1), evaluate *out[i]* as out*[1]*, increment i (i is now 2), do the assignment (*out[0]* = in*[0]*).

C) Evaluate *in[i]* as in*[0]*, evaluate *out[i]* as out[0], increment *i* (*i* is now 1), increment *i* (*i* is now 2), do the assignment (*out[0]* = in*[0]*).

D) The code is compiler dependent, so the compiler carefully computes the best possible answer and then does something else.

E) If you don't write code like this, you won't have to worry about questions like this.

This code is ambiguous, and the actual code generated can change from compiler to compiler. Sometimes the same compiler will generate different code depending on the state of the optimize switch.

The answer, of course, is E.

Ambiguous code is not the only problem that can occur when ++ and -- are used within other statements. The statements

```
i = 2;
s = square(i++);
```

look innocent enough. But square is a macro designed to square a number:

```
#define square(x)        ((x) * (x))
```

If you expanding the macro, you get this:

```
i = 2;
s = ((i++) * (i++));
```

Suddenly you see that i is not incremented once as expected, but twice. And s can be assigned the wrong value. Again, this statement is ambiguous.

You can avoid all these problems by writing the ++ on a separate line:

```
i = 2;
s = square(i);
i++;
```

75

True, putting the ++ inside another statement does make for more compact code, but the value of compactness in C source code is minimal. You're striving for readability and reliability. The one-effect-per-statement rule improves both, especially reliability.

It also simplifies the program. What are the values of *i* and *j* after the following code is executed?

```
i = 0;
j = 0;
x = 0

i = x++;

j = ++x;
```

The increment operator acts differently depending on where it is placed. In front of a variable, the increment is performed before the assignment. Incrementing after causes the assignment to be performed first. So in the example, *i* is 0 (x before increment) and *j* is 2 (x after increment).

This code is a puzzle to some people. But you don't have to remember obscure details like this if you never write code like this. If you simplify the example, it is no longer a puzzle:

```
i = 0;
j = 0;
x = 0

i = x;
x++
x++
j = x;
```

Rule 4-13:
    Avoid side effects.

Rule 4-14:

> Put the operators ++ and -- on lines by themselves. Do not use ++ and -- inside other statements.

Assignments in other statements

C also allows the programmer to put assignment statements inside other statements. For example:

```
/* Poor practice */
if ((result = do_it()) == 5)
    printf("It worked\n");
```

This is another example of a side effect that needs to be avoided. You could just as easily have written this:

```
/* Good practice */
result = do_it();
if (result == 5)
    printf("It worked\n");
```

The second form not only avoids the side effect, but it is simple and clear. The first form is compact, but remember—your goals are readability and reliability.

Unintentional assignments inside other statements can quickly cause trouble. Consider this example:

```
if (result = 5)
    printf("It worked\n");
```

This fragment should print "It worked" only when result is 5. But the code contains a bug. What it actually does is to assign 5 to result, check against 0 (hmm.. no, 5 is not 0 this time), and print unconditionally.

Experienced programmers recognize this as the old = vs == bug. They remember it from the cold, dark night when they stayed up till 2 in the morning staring the bug in the eye a dozen times and not recognizing it the first eleven.

Novice programmers, be warned: you *will* make this mistake, and it *will* cause you a great deal of pain.

This error is so common that now many compilers issue a warning when they see code like this. For example:

```
Borland C++  Version 3.00
Copyright (c) 1991 Borland International

Warning t.c 5:
    Possibly incorrect assignment in function main
```

Rule 4-15:

Never put an assignment statement inside any other statement.

When to use two statements per line

Although there is a rule—One statement per line—don't be fanatical about it. The purpose of the rule is to make the program clear and easy to understand. In some cases, putting two or more statements on one line improves clarity. For example, consider the following code:

```
/* Not as clear as it can be */

    token[0].word = "if";
    token[0].value = TOKEN_IF;

    token[1].word = "while";
    token[1].value = TOKEN_WHILE;

    token[2].word = "switch";
    token[2].value = TOKEN_SWITCH;

    token[3].word = "case";
    token[3].value = TOKEN_CASE;
```

This can easily be rewritten as:

```
/* Clearer */
    token[0].word = "if";      token[0].value = TOKEN_IF;
    token[1].word = "while";   token[1].value = TOKEN_WHILE;
    token[2].word = "switch";  token[2].value = TOKEN_SWITCH;
    token[3].word = "case";    token[3].value = TOKEN_CASE;
```

There is a pattern to this code. The first example obscures the pattern. You can still see it, but it's not as clear as in the second case, which is coded in two statements per line. To make the pattern clearer, the statements are organized in columns.

Rule 4-16:

If putting two or more statements on a single line improves program clarity, then do so.

Rule 4-17:

When using more than one statement per line, organize the statements into columns.

Logic and Indentation

Over the years many people have tried to develop a way to create a document that makes the logic and execution flow of a program easy to understand.

Flowcharts were an early attempt. They presented the program visually by using special symbols to denote things like branch statements, input/output, and termination. Figure 4-1 on the following page shows a sample flowchart. These charts were excellent for small programs, but for programs of normal size they grew too big and bulky. (I remember seeing one that consisted of hundreds of boxes spread across a 6- x 5-foot grid of 11- x 13-inch paper. It took up one whole wall of a conference room. Although it was impressive, no one could understand the whole thing.)

Another problem with early flowcharts was that at the time very few computers could do graphics. (Most couldn't even do lower-case text.) As a result, all flow charts had to be done by hand, and redone if the program changed.

When ALGOL and other structured languages were invented, people discovered that they could use indention to represent levels of control. This is used in C.

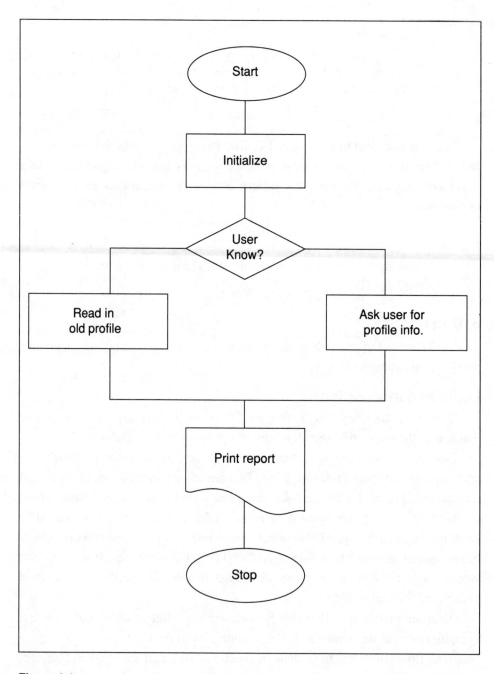

Figure 4-1.

For example:

```
while (count > 0) {
    if (balance[index] == EOF_MARKER)
        count = -1
    else
        total += balance[index];
    index++;
}
```

In this program fragment, you can easily see that the body of the **while** contains both the **if** and the *index++* statement. The statement *count = -1* is indented an extra level, giving a visual clue that it is part of the **if.**

There are several indentation styles, but they all indent one level for each level of logic.

Rule 4-18:

Indent one level for each new level of logic.

Indentation styles

There are many different styles of indentation, and a vast religious war is being waged in the programming community as to which is best. I won't take sides, but I will present the advantages and disadvantages of each style. (Incidentally, the style used throughout this book is the Short Form, chosen only because I'm used to it.)

Short form. In the Short Form, the open brace ({) is put at the end of a line. The text within the braces is indented one level. The close brace (}) is aligned with the beginning of the corresponding statement.

Example:

```
/* Short form indentation */
while (! done) {
    printf("Processing\n");
```

```
        next_entry();
    }

    if (total <= 0) {
        printf("You owe nothing\n");
        total = 0;
    } else {
        printf("You owe %d dollars\n", total);
        all_totals = all_totals + total;
    }

    if (total > 1000)
        printf("You owe a lot\n");
```

The advantage of this style is that it doesn't waste vertical space. The problem is that corresponding braces are not put in the same column. For example, the brace that closes the **while** lines up with the "w" in **while,** not with the brace at the end of the line. This makes it a little more difficult to match braces.

Braces stand alone. In the Braces Stand Alone method, all braces are placed on separate lines:

```
    /* Braces stand alone */
    while (! done)
    {
        printf("Processing\n");
        next_entry();
    }
    if (total <= 0)
    {
        printf("You owe nothing\n");
        total = 0;
    }
    else
    {
        printf("You owe %d dollars\n", total);
        all_totals = all_totals + total;
    }
```

```
if (total > 1000)
    printf("You owe a lot\n");
```

The advantage of this is that the braces are aligned. The disadvantage is that it takes up more vertical space and tends to spread out the code.

Braces indented too. This variation on the Braces Stand Alone method indents not only the statements within the braces, but also the braces themselves:

```
/* Braces indented too */
while (! done)
    {
    printf("Processing\n");
    next_entry();
    }

if (total <= 0)
    {
    printf("You owe nothing\n");
    total = 0;
    }
else
    {
    printf("You owe %d dollars\n", total);
    all_totals = all_totals + total;
    }

if (total > 1000)
    printf("You owe a lot\n");
```

This form of indentation is not as common as the other two. It also has the problem of spacing out the code somewhat.

Variations. One variation on the standard indentation styles concerns **if** statements that affect a single line. For example:

```
if (total > 1000)
    printf("You owe a lot\n");
```

This style of indentation can create confusion, as illustrated by the following example:

```
/* Problem code */
if (index < 0)
    fprintf(stderr,"Error: Index out of range\n");
    exit (8);
```

At first glance, it looks like the program will print an error message and exit only if *index* is out of range. (That's what the programmer intended.) But on closer inspection, you'll notice that there are no braces enclosing the two statements under the **if**. In fact, the code is indented incorrectly.

Indented correctly, the code looks like this:

```
/* Problem code (with a better indent) */
if (index < 0)
    fprintf(stderr,"Error: Index out of range\n");
exit (8);
```

The problem is confusion between multi-line **if** controlled statements and single-line statements. To solve this problem, put single-line statements and their **if**s on the same line:

```
if (total > 1000) printf("You owe a lot\n");
```

This makes very clear that the **if** affects only one line. The problem is that it makes the *printf* line a little more difficult to find and breaks the one-statement-per-line rule.

How much to indent

In this book I indent four spaces for each logic level. Why four? Here are some examples of various indentations.

Two Spaces:

```
while (! done) {
  printf("Processing\n");
  next_entry();
}

if (total <= 0) {
  printf("You owe nothing\n");
  total = 0;
} else {
  printf("You owe %d dollars\n", total);
  all_totals = all_totals + total;
}

if (total > 1000)
    printf("You owe a lot\n");
```

Four Spaces:

```
while (! done) {
    printf("Processing\n");
    next_entry();
}

if (total <= 0) {
    printf("You owe nothing\n");
    total = 0;
} else {
    printf("You owe %d dollars\n", total);
    all_totals = all_totals + total;
}

if (total > 1000)
    printf("You owe a lot\n");
```

Eight Spaces:

```
while (! done) {
        printf("Processing\n");
        next_entry();
}

if (total <= 0) {
        printf("You owe nothing\n");
        total = 0;
} else {
        printf("You owe %d dollars\n", total);
        all_totals = all_totals + total;
}

if (total > 1000)
        printf("You owe a lot\n");
```

The advantage of a smaller indent is that you don't run into the right margin as quickly. The disadvantage is that it's hard to tell the various levels apart.

Larger indents are easier to read, but larger indents mean that you run out of room faster.

Several researchers have studied this problem in detail. They started with the same program and indented it using different indent sizes. They then gave the various flavors of the program to a set of graduate students and told them each to enhance it by adding some additional commands. The students had never seen the program before. The researchers measured time amount of time it took each student to understand and fix the program. As a result of this and other studies like it, they concluded that four spaces is the ideal indentation.

Rule 4-19:
> The best indentation size is four spaces.

Rules

4-1. Write one statement per line.

4-2. Put spaces before and after each arithmetic operator, just like you put spaces between words in English.

4-3. Change long, complex statements into many smaller, simpler ones.

4-4. In a statement that consists of two or more lines, every line except the first must be indented an extra level to show that they are continuations of the first line.

4-5. When writing multi-line statements, put the arithmetic and logical operators at the end of each line.

4-6. When breaking up a line, the preferred split point is where the parenthetic nesting is lowest.

4-7. Align like level parentheses vertically.

4-8. Split long **for** statements along statement boundaries.

4-9. Always split a **for** statement into three lines.

4-10. Write **switch** statements on a single line.

4-11. Keep conditionals on a single line if possible.

4-12. When splitting up a conditional clause (? :), write it on three lines: the condition line, the true-value line, and the false-value line. Indent the last two lines an extra level.

4-13. Avoid side effects.

4-14. Put the operators ++ and -- on lines by themselves. Do not use ++ and -- inside other statements.

4-15. Never put an assignment statement inside any other statement.

4-16. If putting two or more statements on a single line improves program clarity, then do so.

4-17. When using more than one statement per line, organize the statements into columns.

4-18. Indent one level for each new level of logic.

4-19. The best indentation size is four spaces.

## CHAPTER 5

Statement Details

Statements are basic building blocks of a C program, very much as sentences are basic building blocks of English writing. C provides programmers with a rich set of operations, allowing them to easily construct complex and powerful statements. This power must be used judiciously, however. It is far too easy to create complex, unreadable, sometimes indecipherable and unreliable C code. The rules discussed in this chapter will help you create simple, readable, reliable code.

Doing Nothing

One of the most overlooked statements is the "do nothing", or null, statement. The syntax for this statement is extremely simple:

```
;
```

Because it's so tiny, the null statement can easily be missed. For example, the code:

```
for (i = 0; string[i] != 'x'; i++);
```

actually contains two statements: a **for** statement and a null statement. Most people must look closely at this code to find the null statement.

That's bad style. The structure of a well-constructed program is obvious; it does not require close inspection. We need to do something to the null statement to make it obvious, and comment lines easily provide the answer:

```
/* Do nothing */;
```

Now the code fragment looks like this:

```
for (i = 0; string[i] != 'x'; i++)
        /* Do nothing */;
```

With this construction, it is obvious that there are two statements.

Rule 5-1:

> Always put a comment in the null statement, even if it is only
> */* Do Nothing */*.

Arithmetic Statements

C provides the programmer with a rich set of operators. There are 15 precedence rules in C (&& comes before ||, etc.). For example, in this statement:

```
result = 1 << 5 + 1;
```

does the compiler perform the << or the + first? In other words, is the statement equivalent to this:

```
result = (1 << 5) + 1;
```

or to this:

```
result = 1 << (5 + 1);
```

It turns out that + comes before <<, so the second version is correct.

The problem is that all these rules are difficult to remember. I've been programming in C for over 10 years and I can't remember all the rules. I even had to look up the answer to this problem.

Even if you remember all the rules, have pity on the programmer who will be reading your code someday and who may not have your memory. I've devised a practical subset that's simple to memorize:

Rule 5-2:

>In C expressions, you can assume that *, / , and % come before + and -. Put parentheses around everything else.

Following this rule, the problem expression becomes:

```
result = 1 << (5 + 1);
```

and in this statement, the order of operations is obvious.

Function Headings

All C code is contained in functions. The function heading defines its return type and the parameters.

Example:

```
float average(float total, int n_items)
```

There are actually two styles of function declarations. Throughout this book I've been using the newer ANSI-C style. Older compilers allow only the traditional K&R style:

```
float average(total, n_items)
float total;
int n_items;
```

The ANSI-C style is preferred because it is more modern, less error prone, and compatible with C++. Reserve the use of the K&R style for old compilers that don't allow ANSI style declarations.

Rule 5-3:

Use ANSI style function declarations whenever possible.

K&R style parameters

Some of the older C compilers force you to use K&R style parameters. This format does not allow types in the function declaration. The types immediately follow the function declaration:

```
int total(values, n_value)
int values[];
int n_value;
```

Strictly speaking, the declaration *int n_value* is redundant. The type of all parameters defaults to **int**. So you could have written this function as:

```
/* Poor style */
int total(values, n_value)
int values[];
```

The problem with this is the problem that occurs with all defaults: you can't tell the programmer's intent. Did the programmer intend to make *n_value* an integer or leave out a declaration? When you explicitly declare all parameters, you eliminate any doubt.

Rule 5-4:

When using K&R parameters, declare a type for every parameter.

The type declarations for the parameters may be specified in any order. For example, you could have just as easily written this:

```
/* Poor style */
int total(values, n_value)
int n_value;
int values[];
```

The problem here is that you are fighting with the natural one-to-one correspondence between parameters and their type declarations. It's a lot easier to find things if they are put in order.

Rule 5-5:

> When using K&R parameters, put the type declarations for the parameters in the same order as they occur in the function header.

Return type

In C, defining the function type is optional. If the type is not specified, it defaults to **int**. For example:

```
int do_it(void);
```

and

```
do_it(void);
```

are equivalent in C. However, they are not the same to the programmer because the second form is ambiguous. There can be two reasons for not specifying a function type: the return type really should be **int**, or the programmer forgot to define the correct return type.

The explicit declaration of an **int** function type tells the reader of the program, "Yes, this function really does return an **int**."

Rule 5- 6:

> Always declare a function type.

It is possible to have an integer function that doesn't return anything. For example:

```
do_more(void)
{
    /* ...... */
    return;
}
```

Code like this can be found in older programs that pre-date the invention of the **void** type. Good style means that you tell the reader as much as possible. If a function does not return a value, tell the world by declaring a **void** function.

Rule 5-7:

Always declare functions that do not return a value **void**.

Number of parameters

In theory, functions can have any number of parameters. In practice, this is not quite true. That's because while the compilers may be able to handle a function with 100 parameters, programmers cannot.

Long parameter lists remind me of a passage from the UNIX mag tape manual page: "Devices /dev/rmt0, /dev/rmt4, /dev/rmt8, /dev/nrmt0, /dev/nrmt4, /dev/nrmt8 are the rewinding low density, rewinding medium density, rewinding high density, non-rewinding low density, non-rewinding medium density, and non-rewinding high density devices, respectively." The problem with long lists is that you tend to lose track of things.

What's the device name of the "non-rewinding medium density" tape drive? Try to figure it out without counting on your fingers.

Suppose you want to define a function to draw a line. You could write it as this:

```
/* Bad style */
/**********************************************************
* DrawLine — draw a line                                 *
*       draws a line from current point (set by          *
*       GotoPoint to x, y)                                *
*                                                         *
* Parameters                                             *
*       x — Point we draw to (x co-ordinate)             *
*       y — Point we draw to (y co-ordinate)             *
*       style — line style (DASHED, SOLID)               *
*       color — line color (BLACK, WHITE, BLUE...)       *
*       brush — the type of brush to draw with           *
*       pattern — pattern for filling the line           *
*               (STRIPED, CROSS_HATCH, SOLID)            *
*       end_style — how to draw the ends                  *
```

```
*              (CAPPED, FLUSH, ....)                    *
*        front — true if the line is to be drawn over   *
*              everything (false, draw in back)          *
*************************************************************/
void DrawLine(int x, int y,
              style_type style, color_type color,
              brush_type brush, pattern_type pattern,
              end_style_type end_style, boolean front);
```

This is a disaster waiting to happen. All sorts of problems can easily occur. You can forget a parameter, get the parameters out of order, or generally confuse things. Allowing no more than five parameters to a function can help alleviate this.

Rule 5-8:

Allow no more that five parameters to a function.

But now what do you do with the function *DrawLine*? The solution is to take this herd of parameters and stuff them into a structure:

```
struct draw_style {
    style_type style;    /* style for drawing (DASHED, SOLID) */
    color_type color;    /* color (BLACK, WHITE, BLUE...) */
    brush_type brush;    /* the type of brush to draw with */
    pattern_type pattern; /* pattern (STRIPED, SOLID) */
    end_style_type end_style; /* line ends (CAPPED, ....) */
    boolean front;       /* Front or back */
};

/*************************************************************
 * DrawLine — draw a line                                    *
 *      draws a line from current point (set by             *
 *      GotoPoint to x, y)                                    *
 *                                                            *
 * Parameters                                                 *
 *      x — Point we draw to (x co-ordinate)                 *
 *      y — Point we draw to (y co-ordinate)                 *
```

```
*       how — structure describing how to draw the     *
*                line                                  *
*******************************************************/
void DrawLine(int x, int y, struct draw_style *how)
```

There are tremendous advantages to using structures for complex parameter passing. First, it's easier to remember a structure's field name than it is a parameter's position number. (Without looking, can you tell if pattern is the fifth or sixth parameter?)

Another advantage is that you need set only the fields that apply. You can ignore the others. If you used a long parameter list, you must have something for each parameter.

Structures also make it easy to specify default value. For example, if you define the following defaults:

Field	Default Value	Integer value of default
style	DASHED	0
color	BLACK	0
brush	SMALL_ROUND	0
pattern	SOLID	0
end_style	CAPPED	0
front	FALSE	0

then the statement:

```
memset(&current_style, '\0', sizeof(struct style));
```

initializes the entire structure with default values. (Note: For this to work, the defaults must all be zero.)

Passing parameters in globals

Another way of passing parameters to and from a function is to not use parameters at all. Instead, values are passed through global variables. For example, consider the following function:

```
/****************************************************
 * GetToken — read the next token                   *
 *                                                  *
 * Globals used                                     *
 *        in_file — file to get token from          *
 *        token — the token we just got             *
 *        error — 0 = no error                      *
 *                non-zero = error code             *
 ****************************************************/
void GetToken(void)
```

There are many problems with this type of parameter passing. First, it obscures the interface between the function and the outside world. What's the type of *token*? You can't tell. Also, suppose you want to handle multiple files. Then your main code must keep reassigning in_file so that it points to whatever file you are using. For example:

```
in_file = main_file;
GetToken();
main_token = token;

in_file = include_file;
GetToken();
include_token = token;
```

It's much easier to write:

```
main_token = GetToken(in_file, &error);
include_token = GetToken(include_file, &error);
```

A good function interface provides the user with a single, small interface to the function. When parameters are passed as globals, the function interface is divided into two (or more) parts. The global declarations are in on part of the header file and the function declaration in another.

Also, using these types of functions is difficult, requiring multiple statements. It's extremely easy to get things wrong. When you pass parameters as parameters, C checks both the number and type of the parameters. These checks are a big help in improving reliability.

Rule 5-9:

> Avoid using global variables where function parameters will do.

XView style parameter passing

XView programming uses a nearly unique parameter passing style. (It shares this style with the Suntools system from Sun.) For example, the function *XvSet* is defined as:

```
XvSet(handle,
      item, [value], [value], [value], ....
      item, [value], [value], [value], ....
      ....

      NULL);
```

The unique feature of this calling sequence is the use of variable parameter lists. "Item" is a XView attribute. The number of parameters that follow are defined by the attribute.

For example, a typical XvSet function looks like this:

```
XvSet(popup,
  PANEL_CHOICE_NROWS, 5,
  PANEL_CHOICE_STRINGS,
      "Start",
      "Run",
      "Abort",
      "Pause",
      "Continue",
      NULL,
  NULL);
```

The parameter *PANEL_CHOICE_NROWS* is followed by a single number, and *PANEL_CHOICE_STRINGS* is followed by a list of names. This list is terminated by a *NULL*. The entire parameter list is terminated by a *NULL*.

Programmers at Sun went to a lot of work devising this parameter-passing mechanism. It's too bad they came up with something so poor. There are many problems with this style.

First, since the parameter list is variable length and the types of the variables are not fixed, it is impossible to check the type and number of parameters. This defeats any type-checking built into C or *lint*.

The second problem occurs when a terminator is accidentally omitted. In the example, the list of names is terminated by a *NULL*. What would happen if you forgot it?

```
XvSet(popup,
    PANEL_CHOICE_NROWS, 5,
    PANEL_CHOICE_STRINGS,
        "Start",
        "Run",
        "Abort",
        "Pause",
        "Continue",
    NULL);
```

The *XvSet* function reads the parameters, finds the NULL after the strings, and assumes that it ends the strings. *XvSet* thinks more parameters follow, but there are none, so it reads random memory and goes crazy.

It would be much easier to turn the very general *XvSet* into a series of simpler, specialized functions:

```
XvSetPanelNrows(popup, 5);
XvSetPanelChoiceStrings(popup, string_list);
```

This style of parameter passing lets C's type checking do its job and avoids many potential problems.

Rule 5-10:

> Avoid variable length parameter lists. They are difficult to program and can easily cause trouble.

The if Statement

The **if/else** statement presents the programmer with some special problems. The first is ambiguity. There is a small "hole" in the syntax, as illustrated in the following example:

```
if (a)
    if (b)
        printf("First\n");
    else /* Indentation is off */
        printf("Second\n");
```

The question is, which if does the else go with?

A) It goes with if (a)

B) It goes with if (b)

C) The code is ambiguous, so the answer is compiler-dependent.

D) The answer doesn't matter if I don't write code like this.

Give yourself ten points if you answered D. If you don't write silly code, you won't have to answer silly questions. (For the purist, the **else** goes with the nearest **if**. Answer B.)

By using braces, you can avoid the problem of ambiguity as well as make your code clearer.

```
if (a) {
    if (b)
        printf("First\n");
    else
        printf("Second\n");
}
```

Rule 5-11:

> When an **if** affects more than one line, enclose the target in braces.

if/else chains

Frequently programmers need to implement a decision tree. This usually results in a chain of **if/else** statements. Using our current indentation rules, this results in code that looks like this:

```
if (code == ALPHA) {
    do_alpha();
} else {
    if (code == BETA) {
        do_beta();
    } else {
        if (code == GAMMA) {
            do_gamma();
        } else {
            do_error();
        }
    }
}
```

This format adds needless complexity to your program, but how do you simplify it? The solution is to treat the word pair **else if** as a single keyword.

Rewriting the code using this rule results in this:

```
if (code == ALPHA) {
    do_alpha();
} else if (code == BETA) {
    do_beta();
} else if (code == GAMMA) {
    do_gamma();
} else
    do_error();
```

This is at once simpler and easier to understand.

Rule 5-12:

In an **if** chain, treat the words **else** if as one keyword.

if and the comma operator

The comma operator is used to combine statements. For example, the statements:

```
x = 1;
y = 2;
```

are treated as a single statement when written as:

```
x = 1, y = 1;
```

With simple statements, the comma operator is not very useful. However, it can be used in conjunction with **if** to provide the programmer with a unique shorthand.

```
if (flag)
    x = 1, y = 1;
```

This example is syntactically equivalent to:

```
if (flag) {
    x = 1;
    y = 1;
}
```

The problem with the comma operator is that when you use it you break the rule of one statement per line, which obscures the structure of the program.

Rule 5-13:
> Never use the comma operator when you can use braces instead.

The while Statement

Sometimes you want to have a loop go on forever (or until you hit a **break**). There are two common ways of specifying an infinite loop.

```
while (1)
```

and

```
for (;;)
```

The first (**while**) is preferred because it is more obvious and causes less confusion than **for(;;)**. The **while** statement gives the programmer a simple looping mechanism, and because it is so simple there are not a lot of style rules to go with it.

Rule 5-14:
> When looping forever, use **while (1)** instead of **for(;;)**.

Some programmers are tempted to put assignment statements inside a **while** conditional, like this:

```
/* Poor practice */
while ((ch = getc()) != EOF) {
    /* .... */
```

This breaks the no side effects rule. It is compact, but it obscures some of the logic in the code. It is more effectively written like this:

```
/* Good practice */
while (1) {
    ch = getc();
    if (ch == EOF)
        break;
    /* .... */
```

This way, you can see the statements explicitly instead of having to extract them from some cryptic logic.

The do/while Statement

The **do/while** statement is rarely seen in practical C programs. That's because it's redundant—there's nothing that you can do with a **do/while** that can't be done with **while** and **break**.

Because it is so rare, many programmers are surprised when they see it. Some don't even know what to do with it. For these reasons, it is better to simply not use it.

Rule 5-15:

Avoid using **do/while**. Use **while** and **break** instead.

The for Statement

There are two common problems with use of the **for** statement. They can have too little content, or too much.

Missing parts of for loops

The **for** statement is actually three statements in one. Sometimes all three parts are not needed, so one or more is left blank:

```
/* Poor practice */
set_start(&start);

for (;start < end; start++) {
    /* ... */
```

There is a slight problem with this code. We've broken one of rules and did "nothing" silently. The initialization section of the **for** is the empty statement ";".

But with just a ";" to guide you, how can you tell that the programmer didn't accidentally omit the initialization statement? In fact you can't. But including the comment: /* *Start already set* */ tells you the omission was intentional.

```
/* Better practice */
set_start(&start);
```

```
for (/* Start already set */;start < end; start++) {
    /* ... */
```

You also need a comment when there is no conditional clause. For example:

```
for (start = 0; /* break below */; start++) {
    /* ... */
```

Overstuffed for loops

So far we've discussed what happens when you put too little information in a **for** loop. It's also possible to put in too much. As mentioned before, the comma operator can be used to combine statements in an **if**. This also works for the **for** statement. For example, the statement:

```
for (two = 2, three = 3; two < 50; two += 2, three += 3)
```

is perfectly legal. This statement causes the variable *two* to increment by 2 and variable *three* to increment by 3, all in one loop.

The notation is compact and confusing. However, spreading out the loop clarifies the logic:

```
two = 2;
three = 3;
while (two < 50) {

    /* .... */
    two += 2;
    three += 2;
}
```

You'll note that we have also changed the **for** loop to a **while.** It could be left as a **for,** but here the **while** shows the structure of the code more clearly.

Stringing together two statements using the comma operator is sometimes useful in a **for** loop, but such cases are rare.

Rule 5-16:

> Use the comma operator inside a for statement only to put together two statements. Never use it to combine three statements.

The printf Statement

The *printf* function and its cousins are used for outputting the data. The function can be used to print one or more lines. For example:

```
printf("Beginning = %d\nCurrent = %d\n End=%d\n",
            beginning, current, start);
```

Although compact, this obscures what is being output. You are writing three lines, so why not use three *printf* statements?

```
printf("Beginning = %d\n", beginning);
printf("Current = %d\n", current);
printf("Start = %d\n", start);
```

Using this style, you can easily see the structure of the output.

Rule 5-17:

> Use one *printf* per line of output.

Some people might argue that it take more time to do things this way since there are three function calls instead of one. The *printf* function is relatively slow. The amount of overhead in a function call takes 1/1000 of the time it takes to execute even a simple *printf*, so the overhead of the two extra calls in negligible.

Another problem occurs with the use of the *printf*, *puts*, and *putc* functions. If you always use printf, you have consistency. If you use a mixture of *printf*, *puts*, and *putc*, then you increase efficiency at the expense of consistency.

For example:

```
/* Consistent */
printf("Starting phase II\n");
```

```
printf("Size = %d\n", phase_size);
printf("Phase type %c\n", phase_type);

/* Efficient */
puts("Starting phase II\n");
printf("Size = %d\n", phase_size);
puts("Phase type "); putc(phase_type); putc('\n');
```

In most cases, the increase in efficiency is very small. You probably won't notice any speedup in your program unless the code is executed thousands of times in an inner loop. The difference in consistency is extremely noticeable, however. In most cases, readability and consistency considerations outweigh any efficiency considerations.

Rule 5-18:
> Unless extreme efficiency is warranted, use *printf* instead of *puts* and *putc*.

goto and Labels

Good programmers avoid the **goto** statement because it breaks the structure of the program. But every once in a while, even the best programmer needs to use a **goto**.

The **goto** label doesn't fit anywhere in the indentation rules. It's not part of the regular structure, so in order to give it a home, make it stand out, and generally get out of the way, put it up against the left margin.

```
for (x = 0; x < 10; x++) {
    for (y = 0; y < 10; x++) {
        if (data[x][y] == look_for)
            goto found_it;
        }
    }
}
return (NOT_FOUND);

found_it:
```

107

Rule 5-19:

Start **goto** labels in the first column.

The switch Statement

The **switch** statement is the most complex statement in C. It allows the programmer to perform a complex branching operation with a single statement, but sometimes it can be confusing.

Good programming style can make the **switch** statement clearer and more reliable. Consider the following statement:

```
/* Poor practice */
switch (state) {
    case BEGIN_STATE:
        printf("Beginning\n");
    case PROC_STATE:
        printf("Processing\n");
        break;
    case FINISH_STATE:
        printf("Finishing\n");
}
```

At the end of the *BEGIN_STATE* case, there is no **break**, so the program falls through. Thus, when state = *BEGIN_STATE*, you'll get the messages:

```
Beginning
Processing
```

Is this intentional or accidental? From this code, there is no way to know. If the programmer intends a fall through, he or she needs to tell people about it. The comment "/* *Fall Through* */" would help immensely, yielding:

```
/* Not so poor */
switch (state) {
    case BEGIN_STATE:
        printf("Beginning\n");
```

108

```
        /* Fall Through */
    case PROC_STATE:
        printf("Processing\n");
        break;
    case FINISH_STATE:
        printf("Finishing\n");
}
```

Rule 5-20:

> End every case in a **switch** with a **break** or the comment /* *Fall Through* */.

Now consider the last **case**, *FINISH_STATE*. It doesn't need a **break** because it's at the end of the **switch**. However, you may want to consider putting in a **break** to avoid future problems. For example, you may want to add another **case**, perhaps one for *ABORT_STATE*. This would give you this:

```
/* Surprise! */
switch (state) {
    case BEGIN_STATE:
        printf("Beginning\n");
        /* Fall Through */
    case PROC_STATE:
        printf("Processing\n");
        break;
    case FINISH_STATE:
        printf("Finishing\n");
    case ABORT_STATE:
        printf("Aborting\n");
}
```

You may have noticed the error: You need a **break** after the *FINISH_STATE* case. If you get in the habit of always putting in a **break** at the end of a **switch** statement, then you don't have to worry about having to put it in during code modifications.

Good habits are better than a good memory any day.

Rule 5-21:

Always put a **break** at the end of the last case in a **switch** statement.

The **switch** statement now looks like this:

```
/* Almost there */
switch (state) {
    case BEGIN_STATE:
        printf("Beginning\n");
        /* Fall Through */
    case PROC_STATE:
        printf("Processing\n");
        break;
    case FINISH_STATE:
        printf("Finishing\n");
        break;
}
```

But what happens when state is *STATE_IDLE*? There are several possible answers:

1. It is ignored
2. This is a run-time error
3. When you execute this code, state will never contain *STATE_IDLE*, so you don't have to worry about what will happen.

As far as C is concerned, when state is *STATE_IDLE*, then the **switch** is ignored. But that's not good enough. Did the programmer intentionally ignore out-of-range cases, or was it accidental? Again, you don't know. If the programmer intended bad states to be ignored, he or she could have written:

```
default:
    /* Do nothing */
    break;
```

This makes explicit what was implied.

Rule 5-22:

> Always include a **default** case in every **switch**, even if it consists of nothing but a null statement.

But suppose the programmer says that state can never be anything other than the three cases. Do you need a default for something that will never happen?

The answer is a resounding yes! Any experienced programmer will tell you that things that can never happen *do* happen. A good defensive programming technique is to include code for the impossible:

```
default:
    fprintf(stderr,
            "Internal error. Impossible state %d\n",
            state);
    exit (1);
```

So the full-blown switch statement has evolved into this:

```
/* Good style */
switch (state) {
    case BEGIN_STATE:
        printf("Beginning\n");
        /* Fall Through */
    case PROC_STATE:
        printf("Processing\n");
        break;
    case FINISH_STATE:
        printf("Finishing\n");
        break;
    default:
        fprintf(stderr,
            "Internal error. Impossible state %d\n",
            state);
        exit (1);
}
```

Your work on this statement can be summarized with this rule: Always put everything in the **switch** and make it all obvious.

Debug Printing

In spite of all the interactive debuggers, there are still times a programmer needs to use a debugging *printf*. The problem is how to separate the debugging output from the real stuff. One trick is to begin all debug printouts with "##":

```
printf("## state = %d\n", state);
```

This not only makes it easy to identify the debug statements in the log, it also makes it easy to remove them after the program is debugged. All you have to do is search for each line containing "##" and delete it.

Shut up Statements

Always compile your programs will all possible warnings enabled. If you are running under UNIX, run your program through the program *lint*. You want the compiler to find as many potential problems in your code as possible, so you don't have to do it in the debugging stage.

Sometimes you get warnings about things you know about. For example, you might define a variable copyright and never use it. Sometimes the compiler or *lint* will allow you to turn off a warning for a single statement or variable. But sometimes it won't.

For example, there is no way to turn off the "Variable defined but not used" message in the Borland C compiler for a single variable. It's either the whole program or nothing.

The solution to this problem is a set of statements designed solely to turn off warning messages. For example:

```
static char *copyright = "Copyright 1992 SDO";

/* .... */

main()
{
        (void)copyright;      /* Avoid warning */
```

In this case the statement *(void)copyright* "uses" the variable *copyright*. The statement itself does nothing. In fact, the compiler knows it does nothing and generates no code for it. The only reason to put this statement in the code is to trick the compiler into thinking that the variable is being used so it won't issue a warning. Note that a comment is supplied to explain what was done. Otherwise someone looking at this code later might think we're crazy.

The program *lint* gets upset when you don't use the value returned by a function. The case (void) can be used to tell *lint* "I know that this function returns a value, but I don't care."

```
i = get_int();      /* No warning */
get_int();          /* Warning */
(void)get_int();    /* No warning */
```

Rules

5-1. Always put a comment in the null statement, even if it is only */* Do Nothing */*.

5-2. In C expressions you can assume that *, /, and % come before + and - . Put parentheses around everything else.

5-3. Use ANSI style function declarations whenever possible.

5-4. When using K&R parameters, declare a type for every parameter.

5-5. When using K&R parameters, put the type declarations for the parameters in the same order as they occur in the function header.

5-6. Always declare a function type.

5-7. Always declare functions that do not return a value **void**.

5-8. Allow no more than five parameters to a function.

5-9. Avoid using global variables where function parameters will do.

5-10. Avoid variable length parameter lists. They are difficult to program and can easily cause trouble.

5-11. When an **if** affects more than one line, enclose the target in braces.

5-12. In an **if** chain, treat the words **else if** as one keyword.

5-13. Never use the comma operator when you can use braces instead.

5-14. When looping forever, use **while (1)** instead of **for (;;)**.

5-15. Avoid **do/while**. Use **while** and **break** instead.

5-16. Use the comma operator inside a **for** statement only to put together two statements. Never use it to combine three statements.

5-17. Use one *printf* per line of output.

5-18. Unless extreme efficiency is warranted, use *printf* instead of *puts* and *putc*.

5-19. Start **goto** labels in the first column.

5-20. End every **case** in a **switch** with a **break** or the comment */* Fall Through */*.

5-21. Always put a **break** at the end of the last **case** in a **switch** statement.

5-22. Always include a **default** case in every **switch**, even if it consists of nothing but a null statement.

## CHAPTER 6

The Preprocessor

The C preprocessor provides many additional features not found in the language itself. You can use these to create constants, to include data from other files, and to shoot yourself in the foot.

Problems with preprocessors are difficult to spot because they are not obvious. Even the compiler may misreport preprocessor errors. For example, the following program generates an error on Line 5 when the problem is really a bad **#define** statement on Line 1.

```
1:    #define VALUE_MAX   300 ++ 5        /* Problem is here */
2:
3:    void check(int value)
4:    {
5:        if (value > VALUE_MAX) {
6:            printf("Value %d is out of range\n", value);
7:            abort();
8:        }
9:    }
```

Good style is the best defense against preprocessor errors. It is extremely important. By religiously following the rules discussed here, you can catch errors before they happen.*

---

*Religion,** noun. Something a programmer gets after working until two in the morning only to find a bug that wouldn't have been there had he or she religiously followed the rules.

Simple Define Statements

One of the uses of the **#define** statement is to define simple constants. Its format is this:

```
#define SYMBOL value    /* comment */
```

The *SYMBOL* is any valid C symbol name (by convention, **#define** names are all upper-case). The **value** can be a simple number or an expression.

Like variable declarations, a constant declaration needs a comment that explains it. This comment helps create a dictionary of constants.

Some examples:

```
/* Max number of symbols in a procedure */
#define SYMBOL_MAX 500

/* The longest name handled by this system */
#define NAME_LENGTH 50
```

Rule 6-1:

> **#define** constants are declared like variables. Always put a comment that describes the constant after each declaration.

Rule 6-2:

> Constant names are all upper-case.

Constant expressions

If the *value* of a **#define** statement is a compound expression, you can run into problems. The following code looks correct, but it hides a fatal flaw.

```
/* Length of the object (inches) (part1=10, part2=20) */
#define LENGTH  10 + 20        /* Bad practice */

#define WIDTH   30      /* Width of table (in inches) */

/* ..... */
```

116

```
/* Prints out an incorrect width */
printf("The area is %d\n", LENGTH * WIDTH);
```

Expanding the printf line, you get:

```
printf("The area is %d\n", LENGTH * WIDTH);
printf("The area is %d\n", 10 + 20 * WIDTH);
printf("The area is %d\n", 10 + 20 * 30);
```

This another example of how the C preprocessor can hide problems. Clearly, *LENGTH* is *10 + 20,* which is *30*. So *LENGTH* is *30*, right? Wrong. *LENGTH* is literally *10 + 20*, and:

```
10 + 20 * 30
```

is vastly different from:

```
30 * 30
```

To avoid problems like this, always surround all **#define** expressions with parenthesis (). Thus, the statement:

```
/* Length of the object (inches) (part1=10, part2=20) */
#define LENGTH  10 + 20          /* Bad practice */
```

becomes:

```
/* Length of the object (inches) (part1=10, part2=20) */
#define LENGTH  (10 + 20)        /* Good practice */
```

Rule 6-3:

If the value of a constant is anything other than a single number, enclose it in parentheses.

#define constants vs. consts

In ANSI C constants can be defined two ways: through the **#define** statement and through use of the **const** modifier. For example, the following two statements are equivalent:

```
#define LENGTH 10        /* Length of the square in inches */

const int length = 10;   /* Length of the square in inches */
```

Which statement should you use? The **const** declaration is better because it is in the main part of the C language and provides more protection against mistakes. Consider the following example:

```
#define SIZE 10 + 20      /* Size of both tables combined */

const int size = 10 + 20; /* Size of both tables combined */
```

As you've already seen, the **#define** statement is a problem. *SIZE* is a macro and always expands to *10 + 20*. The const int size is an integer. It has the value *30*. So while the statement:

```
area = SIZE * SIZE;     /* Mistake */
```

generates the wrong number, the statement:

```
area = size * size;     /* Works */
```

generates the right number. So the **const** declaration is less error-prone. Also, if you make a mistake in defining a **const**, the compiler generates an error message that points at the correct line. With a **#define**, the error appears when the symbol is used, not when it is defined.

Then why do we have the **#define**? Because early compilers did not recognize const declarations. There is still a lot of code out there that was written for these compilers and that should be modernized.

Rule 6-4:

The use of **const** is preferred over **#define** for specifying constants.

#define vs. typedef

The **#define** directive can be used to define types, such as:

```
#define INT32 long int   /* 32 bit signed integer type */
```

The **typedef** clause can be used in a similar manner.

```
typedef long int int32; /* 32 bit signed integer */
```

The **typedef** is preferred over the **#define** because is better integrated into the C language, and it can create more kinds of variable types than a mere define. Consider the following:

```
#define INT_PTR int *    /* Define a pointer to integer */

typedef int *int_ptr;    /* Define a pointer to an integer */

INT_PTR ptr1, ptr2;      /* This contains a subtle problem */

int_ptr ptr3, ptr4;      /* This does not */
```

What's the problem with the line *INT_PTR ptr1, ptr2*? The problem is that *ptr2* is of type integer, not a pointer to integer. If you expand this line, the problem becomes apparent:

```
INT_PTR ptr1, ptr2;      /* This contains a subtle problem */
/* Expanded */
int *   ptr1, ptr2;      /* This contains a subtle problem */
```

Problems like this can be avoided by using **typedef**.

Rule 6-5:

When possible, use **typedef** instead of **#define**.

Abuse of #define directives

It is possible to use **#define** directives for things other than constants. For example, the macro:

```
#define FOR_EACH_ITEM  for (i = first; i < last; i++)
```

can define a standard **for** loop. This can be used in place of a regular **for**.

```
FOR_EACH_ITEM
    process_item(i);
```

You can even go so far as to create macros that make your C code look like Pascal.

```
#define BEGIN {
#define END }

/* ... */
    if (x == y)
      BEGIN
        /* ... */
      END;
```

The problem with this approach is that you are obscuring the C language itself. The maintenance programmer who comes after you will know C, not a half-Pascal half-C mongrel.

Even the simple *FOR_EACH_ITEM* macro hides vital C code. Someone else reading the program would have to go back to the definition of *FOR_EACH_ITEM* to figure out what the code does. By using the code instead of a macro, no lookup is necessary.

You can easily understand the C code that goes into this:

```
for (i = first; i < last; i++)
    process_item(i);
```

Rule 6-6:

Don't use **#define** to define new language elements.

Keywords and standard functions

Defining new language elements is one problem. A far more difficult problem occurs when a programmer redefines existing keywords or standard routines. For example, in one program, the author decided to create a safer version of the string copy routine:

```
#define strcpy(s1, s1) \
    x_strcpy(s1, s2, sizeof(s1), sizeof(s2))
```

This worked great until the program was ported. Then the program mysteriously bombed at the code:

```
init = 1;

/* This lines hangs the system */
strcpy(name, "noname.c");
```

The programmer performing the port was baffled. There was nothing wrong with the parameters to *strcpy*. And of course, because *strcpy* is a standard function, there shouldn't be a problem with it.

But in this case, *strcpy* is not a standard function. It's a non-standard macro that results in a great deal of confusion.

Think about how difficult it would be to find your way if someone gave you directions like these: "When I say north I mean west, and when I say west I mean north. Now, go north three blocks, turn west for one (when I say one I mean four), and then east two. You can't miss it."

Rule 6-7:

Never use **#define** to redefine C keywords or standard functions.

Parameterized Macros

The **#define** may have arguments. For example, the following macro doubles a number:

```
/* Double a number */
#define DOUBLE_IT(number)        (2 * (number))
```

Enclosing the entire macro in parenthesis avoids a lot of trouble similar to the problems with simple **#define**s.

Rule 6-8:

Enclose parameterized macros in parentheses.

In the next example, the macro *SQUARE* is supposed to square a number:

```
/* Square a number */
#define SQUARE(x) (x * x)
            /* Bad practice,  no () around parameter */
```

The invocation of the macro:

```
a = SQUARE(1 + 3);
```

expands to:

```
a = (1 + 3 * 1 + 3);
```

which is not what was expected. If the macro is defined as:

```
/* Square a number */
#define SQUARE(x) ((x) * (x))
```

Then the expansion will be:

```
a = ((1 + 3) * (1 + 3));
```

So in the second case, $(1+3)^2$ is 16, not 7.

Rule 6-9:

> Enclose each argument to a parameterized macro in parentheses.

Multi-line Macros

The **#define** statement can be used to define code as well as constants. For example:

```
/* Print current values of registers (for debugging) */
#define PRINT_REGS printf("Registers AX=%x BX=%x\n", ax, bx)
```

This is fine as long as the target of the **#define** is a single C statement. Problems occur when multiple statements are defined. The following example defines a macro ABORT that will print a message and exit the system. But it doesn't work when put inside an **if** statement.

```
/* Fatal error found, get out of here */
#define ABORT  printf("Abort\n"); exit(8);

/* .... */
    if (value > LIMIT)
        ABORT;
```

The problem can easily be seen when we expand the macro:

```
if (value > LIMIT)
    printf("Abort\n"); exit (8);
```

Properly indented, this is:

```
if (value > LIMIT)
    printf("Abort\n");
exit (8);
```

This is obviously not what the programmer intended. A solution is to enclose multiple statements in braces.

```
/* Fatal error found, get out of here */
#define ABORT  { printf("Abort\n"); exit(8); }
         /* Better, but not good */
```

This allows you to use the *ABORT* macro in an **if**, like this:

```
if (value > LIMIT)
    ABORT;
```

Unfortunately, it causes a syntax error when used with an **else**:

```
if (value > LIMIT)
    ABORT;
else
    do_it();
```

The **do/while** statement comes to the rescue. The statement:

```
do {
    printf("Abort\n");
    exit(8);
} while (0);
```

executes the body of the loop once and exits. C treats the entire **do/while** as a single statement, so it's legal inside a **if/else** set.

Therefore, properly defined, the macro is:

```
/* Print an error message and get out */
#define ABORT                       \
    do {                            \
        printf("Abort\n");          \
        exit(8);                    \
    } while (0)                  /* Note: No semicolon */

/* ... */
    if (value > LIMIT)
        ABORT;          /* No problem! */
    else
        do_it();
```

Rule 6-10:

Always enclose macros that define multiple C statements in braces.

Rule 6-11:

If a macro contains more than one statement, use a do/while structure to enclose the macro. (Don't forget to leave out the semicolon of the statement).

When macros grow too long, they can be split up into many lines. The pre-processor uses the backslash (\) to indicate "continue on next line." The latest *ABORT* macro also uses this feature.

Always stack the backslashes in a column. Try and spot the missing backslash in the following two examples:

```
/* A broken macro */
#define ABORT                   \
    do {
        printf("Abort\n");      \
        exit(8);                \
    } while (0)
```

```
/* Another broken macro */
#define ABORT \
    do {\
        printf("Abort\n");\
        exit(8);
    } while (0)
```

The mistake in the first example is obvious. In the second example, the problem is hidden.

Rule 6-12:

When creating multi-line macros, align the backslash continuation characters (\) in a column.

Macros and Subroutines

Complex macros can easily resemble subroutines. It is entirely possible to create a macro that looks and codes exactly like a subroutine. The standard functions `getc` and `getchar` are actually not functions at all, but macros. These types of macros frequently use lower-case names, copying the function-naming convention.

If a macro mimics a subroutine, it should be documented as a function. That involves putting a function-type comment block at the head of the macro:

```
/***********************************************************
 * next_char — move a buffer pointer up one                *
 *                                                         *
 * Parameters                                              *
 *     ch_ptr — pointer to the current character           *
 *                                                         *
 * Returns                                                 *
 *     pointer to the next character or                    *
 *     NULL if none                                        *
 ***********************************************************/
#define next_char(ch_ptr) \
    /* ..... definition ........ */
```

Rule 6-13:

Always comment any parameterized macros that look like functions.

The #include Directive

Include files are used to define data structures, constants, and function prototypes for items used by multiple modules. It is possible to put code in an include file, but this is rarely done.

Style for #includes

Most programs put the **#include** directives in a group just after the heading comments. That way they are all together in a known place. System includes (enclosed in <>) come first, followed by any local includes (enclosed in "").

Example:

```
/*********************************************************
 *   ...... heading comments ......                      *
 ********************************************************/
/* System includes */
#include <stdio.h>
#include <alloc.h>
#include <string.h>

/* Local includes */
#include "key.h"
#include "table.h"
#include "blank.h"
```

Rule 6-14:

#include directives come just after the heading comments. Put system includes first, followed by local includes.

#include directives that use absolute file names, that is specify path and name, such as */user/sam/program/data.h* and *Y:\DEVELOP\PROGRAM\DEFS.H* make your program non-portable. If the program is moved to another machine, even one using the same operating system, the source will have to be changed.

The solution is to never use absolute paths. The compiler can be pointed to the correct directory by using the *-I* option. That way you need to change only one Makefile instead of a bunch of source files.

For example:

```
/* Non portable */
#include "/user/sam/program/data.h"

/* Portable, compile with  "-I/user/sam/program" */
#include "data.h"
```

Rule 6-15:

Do not use absolute paths in **#include** directives. Let the *-I* compile option do the work.

Protecting against double #includes

Include files can contain **#include** directives. This means that you can easily include the same file twice. For example, suppose *database.h* and *symbol.h* both need the file *defs.h*. Then, putting these lines:

```
#include "database.h"
#include "symbol.h"
```

in your program brings in two copies of *defs.h*. Defining a structure or type twice can cause errors. So how do you avoid this problem? The solution is to use conditional compilation to prevent the double include from causing trouble.

At the beginning of *defs.h*, insert the lines:

```
#ifndef _DEFS_H_INCLUDED_
#define _DEFS_H_INCLUDED_
```

And at the end, insert this line:

```
#endif _DEFS_H_INCLUDED_
```

The first time through, _DEFS_H_INCLUDED_ is not defined.

The **#ifndef** causes the entire body of the file to be included and causes _DEFS_H_INCLUDED_ to be defined. Therefore, when the file is included again, the **#ifndef** kicks in, and the entire body of the file is now **#ifdef**'ed out.

Conditional Compilation

The preprocessor allows you conditionally to compile sections of code through the use of **#ifdef**, **#else**, and **#endif** directives.

For example:

```
#ifdef DOS
#define NAME "C:\ETC\DATA"
#else DOS
#define NAME "/etc/data"
#endif DOS
```

Actually, the **#else** and **#endif** directives take no arguments. The _DOS_ following them is entirely a comment, but a necessary one. It serves to match the **#else** and **#endif** directive with the initial **#ifdef**.

Note: Some strict ANSI compilers don't allow symbols after **#else** or **#endif** directives. In these cases, the comment _DOS_ must be formally written as /* _DOS_ */.

Rule 6-16:

Comment **#else** and **#endif** directives with the symbol used in the initial **#ifdef** or **#ifndef** directive.

Use conditional compilation sparingly. It easily confuses the code:

```
#ifdef SPECIAL
float sum(float a[])
#else SPECIAL
int sum(int bits)
#endif SPECIAL
{
#ifdef SPECIAL
```

```
        float total;        /* Total so far */
#else SPECIAL
        int total;          /* Total number of bits */
#endif SPECIAL
        int i;              /* General index */

#ifdef SPECIAL
    total = 0.0;
#else SPECIAL
    total = 0;
#endif SPECIAL

#ifdef SPECIAL
    for (i = 0; a[i] != 0.0; i++)
        total += (( bits & i) != 0);
#else SPECIAL
    for (i = 0x80; i != 0; i >> 1)
        total += a[i];
#endif SPECIAL

    return (total);
}
/*
 * A comment explaining that this
 * is bad code would be redundant
 */
```

The structure of this function is nearly impossible to pick out. Actually, it consists of two completely different functions merged together. There are a few lines of common code, but not many.

```
    float sum(float a[])
    {
        float total;        /* Total so far */
        int i;              /* General index */

        total = 0.0;
        for (i = 0; a[i] != 0.0; i++)
```

```
        total += a[i];
    return (total);

}

int sum(int bits)
{
    int total;              /* Total number of bits */
    int i;                  /* General index */

    total = 0;
    for (i = 0x80; i != 0; i >> 1)
        total += (( bits & i) != 0);
    return (total);
}
```

Avoid complex conditional sections. C is difficult enough to understand without confusing the issue. Usually it is better to write two entirely separate but clearer functions.

Rule 6-17:

Use conditional compilation sparingly. Don't let the conditionals obscure the code.

Where to define the control symbols

The control symbols for conditional compilation can be defined through **#define** statements in the code or the *-D* compiler option.

If the compiler option is used, the programmer must know how the program was compiled in order to understand its function. If the control symbol is defined in the code, the programmer needs no outside help. Therefore, avoid the compiler option as much as possible.

Rule 6-18:

Define (or undefine) conditional compilation control symbols in the code rather than using the *-D* option to the compiler.

Put the **#define** statements for control symbols at the very front of the file. After all, they control how the rest of the program is produced.

Use the **#undef** statement for symbols that are not defined. This serves several functions. It tells the program that this symbol is used for conditional compilation. Also, **#undef** contains a comment that describes the symbol. Finally, to put the symbol in, all the programmer needs to do is change the **#undef** to **#define**.

```
#define CHECK   /* Internal data checking enabled */
#undef DEBUG    /* Not the debug version of the program */
```

Rule 6-19:

Put **#define** and **#undef** statements for compilation control symbols at the beginning of the program.

Commenting out code

Sometimes a programmer wants to get rid of a section of code. This may be because of an unimplemented feature, or some other reason. One trick is to comment it out, but this can lead to problems:

```
/*——Begin commented out section——
    open_database();
    update_symbol_table();      /* Add our new symbols */
    close_database();
——End commented out section——-*/
```

Unless your compiler has been extended for nested comments, this code will not compile. The commented-out section ends at the line reading, */* Add our new symbols */*, not at the bottom of the example.

Conditional compilation can accomplish the same thing, with much less hassle.

```
#ifdef UNDEF
    open_database();

    update_symbol_table();        /* Add our new symbols */
    close_database();
#endif UNDEF
```

Note: This will not work if the programmer defines the symbol *UNDEF*. (However, any programmer who defines this symbol should be shot.)

Rule 6-20:

Do not comment out code. Use conditional compilation (*#ifdef UNDEF*) to get rid of unwanted code.

Sometimes the programmer wants to take out a section of code for a few minutes for debugging. This can be done in a similar way:

```
#ifdef QQQ
        erase_backups();
#endif QQQ
```

The symbol *QQQ* was chosen because it is probably not defined and is easy to spot with an editor. This allows all *QQQ* lines to be quickly removed when the bug is found.

Rule 6-21:

Use *#ifdef QQQ* to temporarily eliminate code during debugging.

Rules

6-1. **#define** constants are declared like variables. Always include a comment that describes the constant after each declaration.

6-2. Constant names are all upper-case.

6-3. If the value of a constant is anything other than a single number, enclose it in parentheses.

6-4. The use of **const** is preferred over **#define** for specifying constants.

6-5. When possible, use **typedef** instead of **#define**.

6-6. Don't use **#define** to define new language elements.

6-7. Never use **#define** to redefine C keywords or standard functions.

6-8. Enclose parameterized macros in parentheses.

6-9. Enclose each argument to a parameterized macro in parentheses.

6-10. Always enclose macros that define multiple C statements in braces.

6-11. If a macro contains more than one statement, use the **do/while** trick to enclose the macro. (Don't forget to leave *out* the semicolon of the statement).

6-12. When creating multi-line macros, align the backslash continuation characters (\) in a column.

6-13. Always comment any parameterized macros that look like functions.

6-14. **#include** directives come just after the heading comments. Put system includes first, followed by local includes.

6-15. Do not use absolute paths in #include directives. Let the *-I* compile option do the work.

6-16. Comment **#else** and **#endif** directives with the symbol used in the initial **#ifdef** or **#ifndef** directive.

6-17. Use conditional compilation sparingly. Don't let the conditionals obscure the code.

6-18. Define (or undefine) conditional compilation control symbols in the code rather than using the *-D* option to the compiler.

6-19. Put the **#define** and **#undef** statements for compilation control symbols at the beginning of the program.

6-20. Do not comment out code. Use conditional compilation (*#ifdef UNDEF*) to get rid of unwanted code.

6-21. Use *#ifdef QQQ* to temporarily eliminate code during debugging.

## CHAPTER 7

C++ Style

C++ is an extension of the basic C language. It adds many new features, but the flavor of the old language remains. As far as style goes, everything you've learned so far about C applies to C++, with a few rules added for the new language features.

Comments

There are two types of comments in C++: Traditional C comments, beginning with /* and ending with */; and add new style comments, beginning with // and running to the end of line.

Which should you use? For multi-line comments, use the old style. That way you don't have to keep putting // at the beginning of each line.

```
//**********************************************
// This type of multi-line comment is awkward   *
// because we must begin each line with //.      *
// Not only that, but it looks funny.            *
//**********************************************

/**********************************************
 * Using traditional C comments for boxes like  *
 * this looks nicer and is not as awkward.       *
 **********************************************/
```

For single-line comments, the C++ style (//) is preferred because it leads to fewer errors.

```
/* This code is broken  (total not defined) */
int count;      /* Number of items see so far
int total;      /* Cost of all items */

// This code works
int count;      // Number of items see so far
int total;      // Cost of all items
```

In this example, the first declaration of *count* is missing a closing comment, so the comment engulfs the next line, causing the declaration of *total* to be included in the comment.

C++-style comments go only to the end of line, thereby avoiding hidden multi-line comments. Thus, when you use C++ comments, this problem disappears.

Rule 7-1:

> Use C-style comments (/* .. */) for multi-line comments. Use C++ comments (//) for single-line comments.

Class

The **class** construct allows the programmer to define a set of data along with the procedures that operate on it. For example:

```
// This needs more comments and re-styling
class stack {
    private:
        int data[STACK_MAX];    // Data in the stack
        int current_index;      // Index into the stack
    public:
        stack(void)
        {
            current_index = 0;
        }
```

```
        void push(int value)
        {
            data[current_index] = value;
            current_index++;

        }
        int pop(void)
        {
            current_index-;
            return (data[current_index+1];
        }
    };
```

The first problem is how to handle functions. C++ allows you to declare the complete function inside the class, as shown in the example. Or you can declare only a prototype for the function and put the body elsewhere.

The problem with declaring the entire function in the class is that it makes the class too big. The *stack* class defined is a very simple data type, yet it took 20 lines of code to declare it—and that's without comments. Imagine the amount of text that will be added when you insert a proper function heading for all three procedures.

Keep class declarations small enough so that a programmer can understand them at a glance. This cannot be done if the class is spread over several pages. To keep the class size down to a manageable number of lines, you must move the function bodies to the outside of the class definitions. The class itself contains the prototype and a short one-line comment describing the function. A full description and prototype follow later in the header file.

```
// Better, but not quite right
class stack {
    private:
        int data[STACK_MAX];   // Data in the stack
        int current_index;     // Index into the stack
    public:
        stack(void);           // Create a stack
        void push(int value);  // Push a new element
        int pop(void);         // Pop top element off
};
// ... function definitions
```

This example is much more compact, and it gives the programmer all the required information at a glance. If the programmer wants to know more about a member function, he or she can look further down in the file to locate the function prototype or definition.

Rule 7-2:

Put the function declarations for a class immediately after the class.

Rule 7-3:

Do not put function bodies inside a class declaration. Use a function prototype in the class with a one-line comment. Put the full function body (**inline**) functions or fully commented prototype in the header following the class.

Constructors, destructors, copy and assignment functions

One of the major strengths of C++ is that it hides a great many details concerning data structure management. Four major types of functions are called automatically by C++:

1. constructor (for example, *stack::stack(void)*)
   This function is called every time a class is created.
2. destructor (for example, *stack::~stack(void)*)
   C++ uses this function to destroy a variable when the scope containing the class is exited or when the **delete** procedure is called.
3. copy (for example, *stack (const stack &s)*)
   This function is called when an assignment is made in an initialization statement and for other hidden assignments.
4. assignment (for example, *void operator = (const stack &s)*)
   This function is called when an explicit assignment is made (i.e., *s1 = s2*).

The *stack* example explicitly declared a constructor function, but left out declarations for the destructor, copy, and assignment functions. C++ will supply defaults for these procedures.

Letting C++ supply defaults is fine, but you need to tell the user about it. Otherwise the programmers who come after you won't be able to tell if you intended to use the defaults or just forget to put in the copy and destructor functions.

Therefore, the *stack* class now looks like this:

```
// Finally we got it right
class stack {
    private:
        int data[STACK_MAX];    // Data in the stack
        int current_index;      // Index into the stack
    public:
        stack(void);            // Create a stack
        // ~stack(void);        // Use default destructor

            // Use default copy function
        // stack(const stack &s);

            // Use default assignment
        // void operator = (const stack &s)

            // Push a new element on the stack
        void push(int value);

            // Pop top element off the stack
        int pop(void);
};

// ... function definitions
```

Rule 7-4:

Always declare a constructor, destructor, copy and assignment functions for each class. If you are using the C++ default, then the declaration is a comment. In any case, there is something there for these three vital functions.

Public vs. private

Question: In the following class, is *counter* **public**, **private**, or **protected**?

```
class fun {
    int counter;        // What is this?
    // ......
};
```

Answers:

A) **public**, because the C++ default is **public**.

B) **private**, because the C++ default is **private**.

C) **protected**, because the C++ default is **protected**.

D) If you don't write code like this, you don't have to worry about this question.

Rule 7-5:

Always start a class declaration with the keyword **public**, **private**, or **protected**. Don't depend on defaults.

Nested classes

C++ allows you to declare a structure, union, or class within a class definition. For example:

```
// Nested type example
class array {
    // Used for range checking
    struct range {
        int low;        // Lower bound of the range
        int high;       // Upper bound of the range
    };
    // ... rest of the class
};
```

This type of construction provides good encapsulation and data hiding. The problem is that it adds complexity to the code. In most cases, the problems added by complexity exceed the good done by the added encapsulation. The *array* example could just have easily been written like this:

```
// No nesting, clearer code

// Used for range checking
struct range {
    int low;    // Lower bound of the range
    int high;   // Upper bound of the range
};

class array {
    // .... Array class definition
};
```

Rule 7-6:
Avoid nested class, structure, and union definitions.

Derived classes

A derived class is one that consists of a base class with some additional functionality added. For example:

```
// Basic array
class array {
    public:
        // Stuff an element into the array
        void put(int index, int value);

        // ... and so on
};

// Array with range checking
class check_array : private array {
    public:
        // Stuff an element into the array
```

```
        void put(int index, int value);

        // ... and so on
    };
```

In this example, the range-checking array class (*check_array*) is built from the basic array class (*array*). But there is a problem with the *put* function.

Normally, this code:

```
    check_array data(0, 10);

    data.put(5, -1);
```

would call the function *put* in the base class *array* (*array::put*). But because we have declared our own *put* in the class *check_array*, it overrides the base class's function. In fact, we call *put* in *check_array* (*check_array::put*).

That leads to a question: Did we really want to override the *put* in *array* or did we make a mistake and accidentally pick a name that overrode a function in the base class?

Comments can be used to answer that question.

Rule 7-7:

> When a member function of a derived class overrides a similar function in the base class, put in a comment to indicate that this is intentional.

```
    // Array with range checking
    class check_array : private array {
        public:
            // Stuff an element into the array
            // (override array::put)
            void put(int index, int value);

            // ... and so on
    };
```

Classes and variable declarations

There are two ways of initializing variables. The first is in the declaration:

```
// Initialize in the declaration
int i = 0;
```

The other is through an assignment at the beginning of the function:

```
//Declare but don't initialize
int i;

// Initialize
i = 0;
```

For integers, the difference between these two methods is trivial. For classes, is it significant when you consider what goes on behind your back. For example, consider this code:

```
class array global_array;        // Random global array

void do_it(void)
{
    class array local_array;   //Calls   array::array(void)

    local_array = global_array;
                        //Calls  operator = (global_array)
```

vs. this code:

```
class array global_array;        // Random global array

void do_it(void)
{
    class array local_array = global_array;
        //Calls  array::array(global_array)
```

The first case includes two function calls, the second only one, so the second case is more efficient.

Rule 7-8:

Whenever possible, initialize variables at declaration time.

Setjmp/longjmp problems

C++ does a pretty good job of keeping track of when variables are created and destroyed. There is a hole in its logic, however.

The function *setjmp* marks a place in your code. Later on, a call to the function *longjmp* returns to this location. The call to *longjmp* may be buried under several layers of function calls, but it will restore the stack and jump back to wherever the *setjmp* was invoked.

Although *longjmp* knows enough to restore the stack as it travels up, it does not know to call the destructors for any classes declared.

For example:

```
#include <stdio.h>
#include <setjmp.h>
#include <stdlib.h>

class fun {      // Class for illustration
    int i;
};

void subroutine(jmp_buf);       // A subroutine for testing

int main(void)
{
    int value;              // Value returned by setjmp
    jmp_buf jumper;         // Buffer needed setjmp/longjmp

    // Normally setjmp returns 0.
    // A longjmp, will return to the middle of the setjmp
    //  and return non-zero
    value = setjmp(jumper);
```

```
    if (value != 0) {
        printf("Longjmp with value %d\n", value);
        exit(value);
    }

    printf("About to call subroutine ... \n");
    subroutine(jumper);

    return 0;
}

void subroutine(jmp_buf jumper)
{
    class fun fun;  // A random class
    longjmp(jumper,1);
    // This line is not reached
    // ~fun is never called
}
```

The flow of this program goes like this:

1. Program calls *setjmp* to initialize *jumper*. The function *setjmp* returns 0.
2. *value* is 0 so *subroutine* is called.
3. *subroutine* calls constructor for class *fun*
4. *longjmp* is executed. Program flow takes a hop back to the line

   ```
   value = setjmp(jumper);
   ```

   only this time, *value* is 1.
5. Program exits.

Note that the program never reached the end of subroutine. The destructor for fun was not called.

Rule 7-9:

   Be extremely careful with *setjmp* and *longjmp* in C++. Never use them in functions that declare classes.

Class organization

In summary, a class is organized as:

```
// description of class
class name

        Data declarations
    public:

    Prototypes for constructors
    Prototypes for destructors
    Copy function prototype
    Assignment function prototype

    Other function prototypes
                with one line descriptive comment
};

Full prototypes for member functions
(including heading comments)

For Inline functions include the entire function body
```

Overloading

Overloading occurs when several functions with the same name but different parameter lists are defined. For example:

```
// Heading comments
int max(const int i1, const int i1)
{
    return (i1 < i2 ? i2 : i1);
}

// Heading comments
int max(const float f1, const float f1)
{
    return (f1 < f2 ? f2 : f1);
}
```

In this example, the function *max* returns the larger of two numbers. The particular flavor of *max* selected depends on whether the numbers are integers or floating-point numbers.

In this case, the two versions of *max* are related—that is, they perform the same general function. There is nothing in the C++ language that restricts what you can do with overloaded functions. You could define another flavor of *max* as this:

```
// Very funny max
char max(void)
{
    return ('Q');
}
```

But now you've used max to mean two different things. With two arguments, it returns the maximum of the two. With no arguments, it returns the letter Q. That's confusing.

Rule 7-10:

> When overloading a function, each flavor of the function should perform the same general operation.

C++ allows the programmer to overload not only functions but operators as well. We all know what the + operator does with two integers, but what does it do with two *class foo*'s? C++ lets us answer that question by overloading the + operator:

```
class foo operator + (const foo &f1, const foo &f1)
{
    //... function definition
}
```

When overloading operators, keep it simple. Don't pervert the meaning of an operator. For example, adding two arrays together is a well-defined operation, so overloading + makes sense. Adding *class apples* or *class oranges* does not make sense, so there should be no + operator for these classes.

Rule 7-11:

      Overload operators only if the operation makes sense.

One notable exception to this rule is the streams I/O system. Use of the shift operators (>> and >>), although extremely clever, can be very confusing.

For example:

```
// Very funny code
        cout << 1 << 5;
```

Does this print 1, then 5? Or does it compute *(1 << 5)* and print that number? The operation is confusing. The streams package does make innovative use of overloading to avoid many of the problems with the old I/O system. It does so at the expense of clarity.

I/O Streams

C++ is upwardly compatible with C, so it supports the *stdio.h* I/O library. It also supports a streams-based I/O system. Early versions of the compiler used a slightly different streams system, and many current systems also support the "old streams" system.

So C++ has three separate I/O systems: C style *stdio.h,* Old C++ streams, and C++ streams.

Although each has its own advantages and problems, they don't mix and match.

Rule 7-12:

      Choose one I/O package for your program and stick to it.

Summary

The C++ language builds on the C base and keeps the flavor of the original language. The style rules for C++ are not all that different from those of the original C. All these rules are still built on the same general principles—to make the program as clear and easy to understand as possible.

Rules

7-1. Use C style comments (/* .. */) for multi-line comments. Use C++ comments (//) for single-line comments.

7-2. Put the function declarations for a class immediately after the class.

7-3. Do not put function bodies inside a class declaration. Use a function prototype in the class with a one-line comment. Put the full-function body (**inline**) functions or fully comment prototype in the header following the class.

7-4. Always declare a constructor, destructor, copy and assignment function. If the C++ default is used, these declarations can be just a comment.

7-5. Always start a class declaration with the keyword **public**, **private**, or **protected**. Don't depend on defaults.

7-6. Avoid nested class, structure, and union definitions.

7-7. When a member function in a derived class overrides a similar function in the base class, include a comment that shows that this is intentional.

7-8. Whenever possible, initialize variables at declaration time.

7-9. Be extremely careful with *setjmp* and *longjmp* in C++. Do not use them in functions that declare classes.

7-10. When overloading a function, each flavor of the function should perform the same general operation.

7-11. Overload operators only if the operation makes sense.

7-12. Choose one I/O package for your program and stick to it.

## CHAPTER 8

Directory Organization and Makefile Style

So far we've only discussed the C program itself. This chapter explores the programming environment, which includes organizing your program files, and the *make* utility, which turns source programs into a finished work.

Organizing Your Directories

Small programs consisting of only a few files are easy to organize: just stick everything in one directory. But suppose you're an adventurous programmer and decide to write two programs. Do you stick them both in the same directory? No.

Put each program's files in a separate directory. That way you won't have to figure out which file goes with which program. It also keeps the number of files per directory down to a manageable level.

Rule 8-1:

Whenever possible, put all the files for one program in one directory.

Someday you will probably work on a series of programs, like a set of programs to manage a mailing list. There are programs to enter data, check for duplicates, print labels, and generate reports. All of these programs use a common set of low-level list functions. You can't put each of these functions in each program directory. Duplicate files are very difficult to maintain. You need some way to share files.

The solution is to turn the list functions into a library. The library goes in one subdirectory while other subdirectories hold the various programs.

Suppose you have all four programs all going to the Library directory for their subroutines. But the Library directory contains both the source and the library file (*MAIL.LIB*) and headers (*MAIL.H*) used by these programs. Having access to all that data can easily confuse things. You need to limit what they can see.

The solution is to have a special directory for libraries and header files as illustrated by Figure 8-1. When a library is built it is "released" by placing it in this directory. The header files are put here as well. This directory contains the public part of the library, while the private part stays behind in the source directory.

The top-level directory (*Mailing List*) should be kept free of sources, except for a *Makefile*, *READ.ME*, or other compilation. This makes the files in the top level simple. Adding programs to this level adds unneeded complexity.

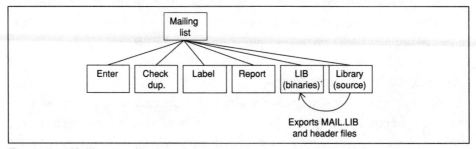

Figure 8-1. Mailing list directory tree

The make Program

Almost all C compilers come with a program-building utility called *make*. It is designed to perform the compilation and other commands necessary to turn source files into a program.

To use *make,* you provide it with a description of your program in a file named *Makefile*. This file also contains the transformation rules that tell it how to turn source into objects.

The *Makefile* is divided into six major sections:

1. Heading comments
2. Macro definitions
3. Major targets
4. Other targets
5. Special compilation rules
6. Dependencies

Heading Comments

The first things a programmer needs to know when confronting a strange *Makefile* are "What does it do?" and "How do I use it?" The heading comments of your *Makefile* should answer those questions.

The first paragraph of the heading comments explains what the *Makefile* creates. For example:

```
##########################################################
# Makefile for creating the program "hello"       #
##########################################################


##########################################################
# This Makefile creates the math libraries:       #
#        fft.a, curve.a and graph.a               #
##########################################################
```

Customization information

Programmers use the preprocessor **#ifdef** to allow for compile-time configuration of their program. For example, there might be a debug version and a production version. Or there might be several different flavors, one for each of the various operating systems the program is designed to run on.

The effect of these conditional compilation directives filter up to the *Makefile*. For example, defining the macro *CFLAGS* as *-DDEBUG* may produce a test program, while the definition *-DPRODUCTION* may produce the production version.

Any configuration information should be listed in the heading comments. This way a programmer can immediately see what customization must be performed on the *Makefile* before he or she starts to build the program.

For example:

```
#
# Set the variable SYSTEM to the appropriate value for your
#        operating system.
#
```

```
#       SYSTEM=-DBSD4_3         For Berkeley UNIX Ver. 4.3
#       SYSTEM=-DSYSV           For AT&T System V UNIX
#       SYSTEM=-DSCO            For SCO UNIX
#       SYSTEM=-DDOS            For DOS (Borland Turbo C)
#
```

Standard targets

The standard form of the *make* command is:

```
make target
```

Here, *target* selects what you want to make. (Microsoft's *make* is a notable exception to this standard.) The programmer needs to know which targets are valid and what they do. Putting a list of targets in the heading provides this information.

For example:

```
#######################################################
# Targets are:                                       #
#       all — create the program "hello"             #
#       clean — remove all object files              #
#       clobber — same as clean                      #
#       install — put the program in                 #
#                       /usr/local/bin               #
#######################################################
```

Over the years a standard set of four targets have developed:

all

This target compiles all the programs. This is the standard default target.

install

This target copies the program and associated files into the installation directory. For local commands this can be */usr/local/bin*. For production software, this will be the official release directory.

clean

> This target removes all program binaries and object files and generally cleans up the directory.

clobber

> Like *clean*, this target removes all derived files—that is, all files that can be produced from another source. In cases where a software control system such as *SCCS* or *RCS* is used, it means removing all source files from the software control system.

lint (UNIX systems)

> This target runs the source files through the program checker

This list represents the minimum "standard" set of targets. Other optional target names have also come into use over the years.

depend or *maketd*

> Creates a list of dependencies automatically and edits them into the *Makefile*. There are several utilities to do this, including a public domain program called *maketd*.

srcs

> Checks out the sources from a software control system such as *SCCS* or *RCS*.

print

> Prints the sources on the line printer.

xrf

> Creates a cross-reference printout.

debug

> Compiles the program with the debug flag enabled.

shar

> Makes a shar-format archive. This format is widely used to distribute sources over the Internet and USENET.

Macro Definitions

The *make* utility allows the user to define simple text macros, such as:

```
SAMPLE=sample.c
```

The macros are used to define a variety of items, such as the source files to be compiled, the compiler name, compilation flags, and other items.

The *make* program predefines a number of macros. (The actual list of predefined macros varies, so check your manual to see which macros are defined for your version of *make*.)

Each macro definition should be preceded by a short, one-line comment that explains the macro. Also use white space to separate each comment/macro combination.

For example:

```
# The standard C compiler
CC = cc

# Compile with debug enabled
CFLAGS = -g

# The source to our program
SOURCE = hello.c

# The object file
OBJECT = hello.o
```

Common macro definitions

There are no standard macro definitions; however, the following is a list of the most common:

CC

The C compiler

CFLAGS

Flags supplied to the C compiler for compiling a single module.

LDFLAGS

Flags supplied to the C compiler for loading all the objects into a single program.

SRCS or *SOURCES*

The list of source files.

OBJS or *OBJECTS*

The list of object files. Some of the newer versions of *make* have an extension that allows you to automatically generate this macro from the *SRCS* macro. For example, the following line tells Sun's *make* that *OBJS* is the same as *SRCS*, except change all the .c extensions to .o.

```
OBJS = $(SRCS:.c=.o)
```

HDRS or *HEADER*

The list of header files.

DESTDIR

The destination directory, where the *install* target puts the files.

Configurable variables

As mentioned earlier, macros are frequently used for configuration information. When it comes to actually defining the variable, it is useful to list all the definitions and then comment all but the selected one. For example:

```
# Define one of the following for your system
SYSTEM=-D4_3            # For Berkeley UNIX
```

```
#SYSTEM=-DBSD4_3        # For Berkeley UNIX Version 4.3
#SYSTEM=-DSYSV          # For AT&T System V UNIX
#SYSTEM=-DSCO           # For SCO UNIX
#SYSTEM=-DDOS           # For DOS (Borland Turbo C)
```

Major Targets

So far, we've just been defining things. At this point it's time to tell *make* to actually do something. This section contains the rules for all the major targets listed in the comment header. These targets are grouped just after the macros so they can be easily located.

For example:

```
all: hello

install: hello
        install -c hello /usr/local/bin

clean:
        rm -f hello.o

clobber: clean
```

Other Targets

Often a *Makefile* contains several intermediate or minor targets. These are to help build things for the major targets. For example, the major target *all* calls upon the minor target *hello*.

Minor targets follow the major ones.

Example:

```
hello: $(OBJECTS)
        $(CC) $(CFLAGS) -o hello $(OBJECTS)
```

Special Rules

The *make* program knows about all or most standard compilers, such as the C compiler. Sometimes you need to define a rule for a special compiler, such as the parser generator *yacc*. This program takes grammars (y files) and turns them to C code.

The *Makefile* rule for this program is:

```
#
# Use yacc to turn xxx.y into xxx.c
#
.y.c:
        yacc $*.y
        mv yacc.xx.cc $*.c
```

Notice that every special rule has a comment explaining what it does.

This target section can also be used to override the default rules. For example, if *all* your C files need to run through a special pre-processor, you can install your own rule for C compilation:

```
#
# Run the files through "fixup" before compiling them
#
.c.o:
        fixup $*.c
        $(CC) $(CFLAGS) -c $*.c
```

Some *make* programs provide you with a default rule file. **Under no circumstances should you change this file.** Doing so changes causes *make* to behave in a non-standard way. Also, programmers expect the complete compilation instructions to be kept in the program's *Makefile*, not hidden in some system file.

Dependencies

The dependencies section shows the relationship between each of the binary files and their source. For example:

```
hello.o: hello.c banner.h
```

tells *make* that *hello.o* is created from *hello.c* and *banner.h*.

Dependency checking is the weakest point in the *make* command. Frequently this section is out of date or missing entirely. Advanced *make* programs have an automatic dependency checking, thus eliminating the need for this section.

Other solutions have also sprung up. The public domain utility *maketd* and other similar programs automatically generate dependency lists. They all depend on this section being at the end of the *Makefile*.

Example

The full *Makefile* for the *hello* program is:

```
###############################################################
# Makefile for creating the program "hello"          #
# Set the variable SYSTEM to the                     #
# appropriate value for your                         #
#         operating system.                          #
#                                                    #
# SYSTEM=-DBSD4_3   For Berkeley UNIX Version 4.3    #
# SYSTEM=-DSYSV     For AT&T System V UNIX           #
# SYSTEM=-DSCO      For SCO UNIX                      #
# SYSTEM=-DDOS      For DOS (Borland Turbo C)         #
#                                                    #
# Targets are:                                       #
#        all - create the program "hello"            #
#        clean - remove all object files             #
#        clobber - same as clean                     #
#        install - put the program in                #
#                         /usr/local/bin             #
###############################################################
#

# Macro definitions
#

# The standard C compiler
CC = cc

# Compile with debug enabled
CFLAGS = -g
```

```
# The source to our program
SOURCE = hello.c


# The object file
OBJECT = hello.o

# Define one of the following for your system
SYSTEM=-D4_3            # For Berkeley UNIX
#SYSTEM=-DBSD4_3        # For Berkeley UNIX Version 4.3
#SYSTEM=-DSYSV          # For AT&T System V UNIX
#SYSTEM=-DSCO           # For SCO UNIX
#SYSTEM=-DDOS           # For DOS (Borland Turbo C)


# Compile with debug enabled
CFLAGS = -g $(SYSTEM)

#
# Major targets
#
all: hello

install: hello
        install -c hello /usr/local/bin

clean:
        rm -f hello.o

clobber: clean

#

# Minor targets
#
hello: $(OBJECTS)
        $(CC) $(CFLAGS) -o hello $(OBJECTS)

#
# No special rules
#
```

```
#
# Dependencies
#
hello.o: hello.c banner.h
```

Common Expressions

Whenever possible, use macros for common directories or other text. For example:

```
#
# Poor practice
#
INSTALL_BIN = /usr/local/bin     # Place to put the binaries
INSTALL_MAN = /usr/local/man     # Place to put the man pages
INSTALL_HELP = /usr/local/lib    # Place to put help info.


#
# Better practice
#
DESTDIR=/usr/local
INSTALL_BIN = $(DESTDIR)/bin      # Place to put the binaries
INSTALL_MAN = $(DESTDIR)/man      # Place to put the man pages
INSTALL_HELP = $(DESTDIR)/lib     # Place to put help info.
```

and

```
#
# Poor practice
#

# Yacc switches
YACC_FLAGS = -c -t -I/project/include -I/general/include

# C switches
CFLAGS = -c -g -I/project/include -I/general/include
```

```
#
# Good practice
#

INCLUDES=-I/project/include -I/general/include

# Yacc switches
YACC_FLAGS = -c -t $(INCLUDES)


# C switches
CFLAGS = -c -g $(INCLUDES)
```

Complexity

Installing a program can be tricky. I've seen a shell script with more than 100 lines created just to install a single program. There is a temptation to put long, complex command sets into the *Makefile*. Because of the difficulties of both shell program and *Makefile* format, this results in a large, complex, and impossible-to-maintain piece of code.

In general, it is best to put large command scripts in a batch file. This makes it easier to test, debug, and comment them.

Portability Considerations

*Makefile*s have a standard format that is portable across most systems. However, compile time options differ from system to system. For example, a program written to work on both UNIX and DOS will require two entirely different commands sets to create it. Stuffing two sets of compilation instructions in a single *Makefile* can get messy. When this happens, it is best to create a separate *Makefile* for each system. The standard method for naming these various *Makefile*s is *<system>.mak*. Some standard names are:

```
bsd.mak              BSD 4.3 UNIX Makefile
att.mak              AT&T System V
sun.mak              SUNOS UNIX system
turboc.mak           DOS using Borland's Turbo C
msc.mak              DOS using Microsoft's C compiler
sco.mak              SCO UNIX
```

This list can grow quite long as programs are ported to more and more systems. A *read.me* file must be distributed with the software to describe how to select the proper *Makefile*.

Generic Makefiles

Some of the more advanced *make* commands have an include facility that allows the inclusion of other files in the *Makefile*. Some programmers have tried to create generic *Makefile*s, to be used like this:

```
#
#  Define some macro names to be
#     used by the generic Makefile
#
SRCS=hello.c
OBJS=hello.o
PROGRAM=hello


include(Makefile.generic)
```

In theory, this should work nicely. There is one generic *Makefile* that does everything, then all you have to do is set things up properly.

In practice, though, it's not so simple. Creating a program is never a standard process and far too many have their little peculiarities. Trying to program around them in a generic *Makefile* is extremely tricky.

One approach is to create a generic *Makefile* to be used as a template for making custom *Makefile*s. The problem with this approach is that when you want to add a new target to every *Makefile*, you must edit each one.

The solution? There isn't one. This is a classic tradeoff of standardization vs. flexibility. Generic *Makefile*s are standard but inflexible. Individual *Makefile*s are flexible but hard to standardize.

Conclusion

*Makefile*s are as important to the programming process as the program itself. A well-designed *Makefile* makes it easy to create a program. Comments are necessary to tell programmers the vital information that lets them create future versions of your program.

Rule

8-1. Whenever possible, put all the files for one program in one directory.

## CHAPTER 9

User-Friendly Programming

So far we've discussed the use of style to make your code clear and easy to read. But style doesn't stop at the printed page. A program is not only edited, debugged, and compiled; it is also used. In this chapter we extend our discussion of style to include how the program appears when it is in use.

What Does User-Friendly Mean?

As programmers, we encounter a large number of tools, utilities, and other programs. Some are a joy to use, letting us get our work done with a minimum of fuss. Others are a nightmare, with obscure and complex command sets.

What is a user-friendly program? Simply a program that the user considers a friend instead of an enemy.

In the early days of computing, machines cost millions of dollars and programmers cost only a few thousand. Companies could afford to keep several specialists around to translate management requests into language the computer could understand.

For the programmers, the early computers were very user-unfriendly. IBM's OS/360 required the programmer to interface with it using a particularly brutal language called JCL. The commands were cryptic; for example, "copy" was "IEBGENER", and specifying a file could easily take up three to five lines of JCL code.

Over the years, computers have dropped in price, and the cost of programmers has increased. Low prices have meant that more and more people can buy computers. High salaries have meant that fewer and fewer people can afford to pay a full-time programmer to run them.

Software has had to evolve with the times, too. Programs have had to become easier to use in order to accommodate newer, less computer-literate clients.

Today, people with no computer training at all can go into Radio Shack, plunk down $1000 and walk out with a computer that is faster and more powerful than an early IBM that cost millions of dollars.

Law of Least Astonishment

For years, people have tried to come up with a set of laws to define what is user-friendly and what is not. Many of them involve complex standards and lots of rules; but the best law that I've seen governing program design is the Law of Least Astonishment: the program should act in a way that least astonishes the user.

Rule 9-1:

Law of Least Astonishment: The program should act in a way that least astonishes the user.

Modeling the User

Computers intimidate many people. (Those who aren't intimidated tend to become programmers.) Your first step in writing a user-friendly program is to put yourself in the shoes of the user. What does a user want from the system?

Always remember that users have a job to do. They want the computer to do that job their way, with a minimum of effort.

Almost all tasks done by computer were at one time done by hand. Before word processing, there was the typewriter. Before databases, there was the card file. A good program should be designed to emulate a manual task that the user knows. For example, a good word processor lets the user treat it like a typewriter. True, it adds a great many features not found on a typewriter, but at heart it still can be used like a typewriter.

A good example of a program imitating a manual procedure occurred when a business school graduate student was attending a financial analysis class. He noticed that the professor had a set of figures arranged in a neat set of rows and columns on the blackboard. Every time the teacher changed one number, he had to recalculate and write a new set of numbers.

The student figured that a computer could perform the work automatically, so he invented VisiCalc, the first spreadsheet program. Successful modeling brought this observant programmer a million-dollar idea.

Error Messages

Sooner or later, every user makes a mistake. When that happens, an error message usually appears. Writing a good error message is an art. Care and thought need to go into the creation of these messages.

Examples of poor error messages abound. I once ran a FORTRAN program and was surprised to see the following message at the end of my run:

```
JOB KILLED BY IEH240I
```

So I consulted the book called *Messages and Codes* (aka *The Joke Book*), which was supposed to contain a complete list of errors, and it did—for all the codes except the IEH series, which was in the FORTRAN manual. Going to the FORTRAN book, I discovered that IEH240I meant "Job killed by fatal error." Of course, I knew it was a fatal error the moment it killed my job.

It turns out that the program tried to do a divide by 0, which resulted in a "Divide by 0" message followed by the IEH240I.

Error messages should not be cryptic. The IEH240I code sent me on a wild goose chase through two books, only to wind up where I started.

You cannot expect the user to know computer terminology. For example, a message like this:

```
FAT table full
```

means nothing to most users. "What do I do? Put the computer on a diet?"

Remember that most users are not programmers, and they won't think like programmers. For example, a secretary was having trouble saving a memo and complained to the computer center. "Do you have enough disk space?" asked the programmer. The secretary typed for a second and said, "Yes, I see a message disk space OK." The programmer looked at the screen, and sure enough, there was the message:

```
    Disk space: OK
```

After a few files were deleted, the message read:

```
    Disk space: 16K
```

and the secretary was able to save the memo.

Sometimes an error message baffles even experienced programmers. For example, I'm still trying to figure out this one:

```
    Error: Success
```

Sometimes it is difficult to pick out the error messages from all the other noise being produced by the computer. A solution is to clearly identify error messages by starting them with the word *Error:*.

A good error message tells the user what's wrong in plain English, and suggests corrective action. For example:

```
    Error: Disk full.
    Delete some files or save the data on another disk.
```

Rule 9-2:

Begin each error message with *Error:*. Begin each warning message with *Warning:*.

The classic IBM PC self test follows this rule, sort of:

```
Error: Keyboard missing
Press F1 to continue
```

One student programmer who took particular pride in his program created a work with the most interesting and obsequious error message I've seen:

```
This humble program is devastated to report that it cannot
accept the value of 200 for scale because the base and thought-
less programmer who implemented this program has thoughtlessly
limited the value of scale to between 0.01 and 100.0. I implore
your worthiness to reduce the scale and run this miserable pro-
gram again.
```

The Command Interface

MS/DOS has a very strange command interface. It appears to be built out of bits and pieces stolen from other operating systems, which results in a command language that is far from consistent.

For example, to get rid of a file, you use the command ERASE. But to get rid of a directory, the command is RMDIR. This is one of the many reasons MS/DOS is considered user-unfriendly. The command interface should be consistent. If you are going to use ERASE to get rid of a file, use ERASEDIR to get rid of a directory.

The GNU *ispell* program is another example of a program with a problem in consistency. This program checks spelling, and when it detects a misspelled word it produces a numbered list of suggested corrections:

```
Misspelled word:       Oualline

1.     Hauling
2.     Mauling
3.     Pauling
```

To select a replacement, you just type in the number. Type a 2, and "Oualline" becomes "Mauling." The problem is that there can be more than 10 suggestions. In such cases, 1 is ambiguous. It can mean 1 or the first digit of 10. So the program forces you to type <ENTER> if you really want to select 1. Let's review the command interface:

>To select a word, type its number, unless there are more than 10 displayed and you want number 1, then type the number 1 and <ENTER>.

How much simpler it would be to say:

>Type the number and <ENTER>.

This example demonstrates the main strength of consistency: You don't have to remember very much. With computer manuals consisting of 1000+ pages, you must have consistency or you'll get insanity.

Help

Early programs were designed to save disk and memory space, not to be user-friendly. It was difficult to get more than code out of them, much less a help screen.

As user-friendly programming has gained acceptance, help systems have improved as well. Today there are help compilers to aid the programmer produce context-sensitive help screens. The compiler also allows the programmer to embed cross-references in the text that let the user jump immediately to a related subject. Finally, there is an index of all topics that the user can search.

Help compilers are available for Borland's compiler and Microsoft's Windows development system. But even without a help compiler, every program needs to provide some help. More complex programs need context-sensitive help. Far too often, help systems are not designed into programs from the start, but instead as "if we have time" projects. This makes programs very unfriendly.

Safety Nets

Occasionally a user will try to do something that causes permanent damage or loss of data to their system. A user-friendly program provides users with a safety net preventing them from doing something stupid unless they really want to.

For example, if the user tries to write over an existing file, the message:

```
About to overwrite the file START.TXT.
Are you sure [n]?
```

This gives the user a chance to abort the operation without damage.

Rule 9-3:
> Don't let users do something stupid without warning them.

Accelerators

Some users eventually develop into power users. You know the type—they know every command in the program, have an amazing set of tricks for getting around program limitations, and can quote long passages from the reference manual.

The user interface for the power user is different from that needed by the novice. Many programs provide accelerator keys, which allow the user to perform common commands with a single keystroke. For example, to run a program in the Borland C compiler you must type Alt-R to bring up the run menu, and then R to run the program. Power users can hit Control-F9.

Rules

9-1. Law of Least Astonishment: The program should act in a way that least astonishes the user.

9-2. Begin each error message with *Error:*. Begin each warning message with *Warning:*.

9-3. Don't let users do something stupid without warning them.

## PART II

Style Manual

Style Manual

This is a style manual for C programmers. These rules are designed to help the programmer create reliable, easily maintained code.

Golden Rule of Programming

Make your program as clear and easy to read as possible.

The rules presented in this book are an aid, not a straightjacket, to writing good programs. If a rule gets in the way of writing a good program, feel free to break it.

General Program Design

Design your program like a reference book. Reference books generally do a very good job of presenting information in an organized, understandable format.

Modules consist of two parts: a header file and the code. The header file contains all the information needed to use the function. The code section actually does the work.

File Basics

Source file rules:

- Keep programs files no longer than about 2,000 to 3,000 lines.
- Do not use lines that are longer than 80 characters. A limit of 72 characters is even better. (It allows room for numbered listings.)
- Use 8-character tab stops.
- Use only the 95 standard ASCII characters in your programing. Avoid exotic characters.

Comment Types

Program files are limited to a monospaced, one-font character set. But even with these limitations, programmers can use their imagination to create a variety of commenting styles:

Boxed comments

```
/*********************************************************
 * This is a boxed comment.  The box draws attention     *
 * to it.  This type of comment is used for program,     *
 * module and function headings.                         *
 *********************************************************/
```

```
/*------------------------------------------------------*\
 * Another box style                                     *
\*------------------------------------------------------*/
```

Section markers

```
/* >>>>>>>>> Major Section Marker <<<<<<<<<< */
```

```
/* ---------- Minor Section Marker ---------- */
```

Important warnings

```
/*********************************************************
 *********************************************************
 ********** Warning:  This is a very important **********
 ********** message.  If the programmer misses **********
 ********** it, the program might crash and     **********
 ********** burn.  (Gets your attention         **********
 ********** doesn't it.)                         **********
 *********************************************************
 *********************************************************/
```

Smaller section headers

```
/*
 *      * ============== *
 *      * Section Header *
 *      * ============== *

 */
```

In-line comments

```
static int count = 0;    /* A simple end of line comment */

/* This was an end of line comment that grew too long */
static int total = 0;

main(void)
{
    /* This is an in-line comment */

    total++;

    /*
     * This is a longer in-line comment.
     * Because it is so verbose it is split into two lines.
     */
    return (0);
}
```

Making a single word stand out

```
/*
 * This is a sentence with **one** word emphasized.
 */
```

Graphics

```
/************************************************************
 * Format of address menu                                  *
 *                                                         *
 *      <--- MENU_WIDTH -------->           MENU_HEIGHT    *
 *      +-----------------------+                 ^        *
 *      | Name:_____   |<--- NAME_LINE   |        *
 *      | Address:_____   |<--- ADDR_LINE   |        *
 *      | City_____    |<--- CITY_LINE   |        *
 *      | State:___  Zip:____   |<--- STATE_LINE  |        *
 *                                                         *
 *      +-----------------------+                 V        *
 *          ^          ^                                   *
 *          |          |                                   *
 *          |          +---- ZIP_X                         *
 *          +--- BLANK_X                                   *
 ************************************************************/
```

Singling out bits in a byte or word

```
/************************************************************
 * Line Control Register                                   *
 *       for the PC's COM ports                            *
 *                                                         *
 *      76543210                                           *
 *      XXXXXXXX                                           *
 *      ^^^^^^++----- Number of data bits                  *
 *      |||||+------- Number of stop bits                  *
 *      ||+++-------- Parity control                       *
 *      |+----------- Send Break                           *
 *      +------------ Mode control                         *
 ************************************************************/
```

Program Headings

A program heading introduces the program. A list of sections that can be used for a program heading follows.

Purpose

An explanation of why the program was written and what it does.

Author

Your name.

Copyright or License

The information required by the lawyers.

Warning

Any information the programmer should be warned about.

Usage

A short description of how to use the program.

Restrictions

The limitations of the program.

Algorithms

Any algorithms that are special or nonstandard.

References

Where algorithms or other information was obtained.

File Formats

How input or output files are formatted.

Revision History

A list of revisions, including who did them and what was done. (Sometimes this information is kept by a revision control system.)

Notes

A catch-all for any other information you may want programmers to know in the future.

Kitchen Sink

Actually, you shouldn't include the kitchen sink. Remember that every section you include must be input and maintained. That means work, so limit yourself to only the sections that are really useful.

The following is an example of a streamlined program heading.

```
/**********************************************************
 * lab -- handle the labeling of diskettes               *
 *                                                        *
 * Usage:                                                 *
 *      lab -w <drive>:<name>    Write label to disk      *
 *      lab -r <drive>:          Read label               *
 *      lab -c <drive>: <drive>: Copy label.              *
 *                                                        *
 *      Copyright 1992 Steve Oualline                     *
 **********************************************************/
```

Module headings

Module headings contain the same information as program headings, except there is no Usage section. Sometimes there is a section listing all the functions in the module. This list usually requires too much work to maintain and is frequently omitted. You can easily get a list of functions from the module's header file.

```
/**********************************************************
 * symbol.c -- Symbol table routines                     *
 *                                                        *
 * Author: Steve Oualline                                *
 *                                                        *
 * Copyright 1992 Steve Oualline                          *
 *                                                        *
 * Warning: Running out of memory kills the program       *
 *                                                        *
 * Algorithm:                                             *
 *      The symbol table is kept as a balanced binary     *
 *      tree.                                             *
 **********************************************************/
```

Function headings

A function heading includes:

Name/description

The name and a short description of the function.

Parameters

A list of parameters, one per line, with a short description of each one.

Return value

The value that the function returns.

```
/***********************************************************
 * find_lowest -- find the lowest number in an array       *
 *                                                         *
 * Parameters                                              *
 *     array -- the array of integers to search            *
 *     count -- number of items in the array               *
 *                                                         *
 * Returns                                                 *
 *     the index of lowest number in the array             *
 *     (in case of a tie, the first instance of the        *
 *     number)                                             *
 ***********************************************************/
int find_lowest(int array[], int count)
```

When to Write Comments

Always write comments when you are creating the code. That's when you best know what you're doing. If you wait till later to put them in, you'll forget things. Also, far too often, you'll never find time later.

Variables

Use simple, descriptive variable names:

```
/* Bad names */
q              i              zz
knt            f_rfs  p


/* Good names */
line_number    biggest_size   account_balance
amount_owed    last_entry     total
```

Good variable names can be created by using one word or by putting two or three words together, separated by an underscore (_).

Never use a lowercase L or upper- or lowercase O for variable or constant names.

Don't use the names of existing C library functions or constants.

```
/* Bad variables and good constants */
l    1    0    0       /* Guess which ones are numbers */
```

Use similar names for variables that perform similar functions.

```
/* Good names */
int largest_balance;
int smallest_balance;
int average_balance;
```

Don't use variable names that differ by only one or two characters. Variable names should be obviously different.

```
/* Bad names */
int total;    /* Total for current entry */
int totals;   /* Total for all entries */

/* Better names */
int current_total;        /* Total for current entry */
int all_total;            /* Total for all entries */
```

Standard prefixes and suffixes for variables include:

_ptr   Pointer
_p   Pointer (The suffix *_ptr* is preferred)
_file   A FILE type variable
_fd   A file descriptor returned by *open* or *create*
*n_*   Number of

```
/* Examples of standard prefixes/suffixes */

struct data *last_ptr;      /* Pointer to last data element */
struct user *user_p;        /* Pointer to current user data */
FILE *in_file;              /* File to read data from */

/* File descriptor for word database */
int word_fd;

struct entry entries[];      /* Database records */
int n_entries = 0;          /* Number of database records */
```

When creating a two-word variable name where the words can be in any order, always put the more important word first.

```
/* Poor variable names */
int max_entries;
int max_amount;

/* Better */
int entry_max;
int amount_max;
```

Short names such as *x, y,* and *i* are acceptable when their meaning is clear and when a longer name would not add information or clarity.

```
/* These names are OK */
int x; /* Current location on screen, x dir (pixels) */
int y; /* Current location on screen, y dir (pixels) */
int i; /* General purpose temporary index */
```

Use *argc* for the number of command line arguments and *argv* for the argument list. Do not use these names for anything else.

```
/* Never program like this */
int main(int ac, char **av)

/* Program like this */
int main(int argc, char *argv[])
```

Follow every variable declaration with a comment that defines it.

Whenever possible, include the units of measure in a variable's description.

```
/* Good practice */
int    total; /* Total number of all entries */
float average;/* Average time to do record (seconds) */
char line[80];/* Line we just read from the input */
int length;   /* Length of the current line (characters) */
```

Name and comment each field in a structure or union like a variable.

Begin each structure or union definition with a multi-line comment that defines it.

Put at least one blank line before and after a structure or union definition.

```
/* Good practice */

int n_entries;        /* Number of items in "entries" */

/*
 * account_entry -- data for a single account
 *                         transaction
 */
struct account_entry {
    int amount;       /* Amount of the transfer (pennies) */
    int balance;      /* Balance after transfer (pennies) */
    int from_account;/* Where we got the money */
    int to_account;/* Where it went */
};

FILE *in_file;        /* File to get account data from */
```

When you can't put a descriptive comment at the end of a variable declaration, put it on a separate line above. Use blank lines to separate the declaration/comment pair from the rest of the code.

```
/* Good practice */

int short_var;        /* Description is short */

/* This description is much longer and verbose */
int long_var;

int another_var;      /* Another short description */
```

Group similar variables together. When possible, use the same structure for each group.

```
int start_hour;       /* Hour when the program began */
int start_minute;     /* Minute when the program began */
int start_second;     /* Second when the program began */
```

Don't use hidden variables.

```
/* Bad practice */

int count;    /* Number of data entries */

int funct(void)
{
    float count;      /* Hidden variable */



/*--------------------------------------------*/
/* Better */
int count;    /* Number of data entries */

int funct(void)
{
        float our_count;      /* --Different name-- */
```

Portable Types

When defining portable types, avoid ambiguous names like *WORD* and *DWORD*. A good set of names is *INT16*, *INT32*, *UINT16,* and *UINT32*.

Numbers

Floating-point numbers must have at least one digit on either side of the decimal point.

The exponent in a floating-point number must be a lower-case e. This is always followed by a sign.

```
/* Bad numbers */
.5      8.      1E33


/* Good numbers */
0.5     8.0     1.0e+33
```

Start hexadecimal numbers with *0x*. (Lower-case x only.)
Use upper-case A through F when constructing hexadecimal constants.

```
/* Bad numbers */
0X123  0Xace  0Xfeed

/* Better numbers */
0x123  0xACE  0xFEED
```

Long constants must end with an upper-case L.

```
/* Bad numbers */
12321  11      331

/* Good numbers */
1232L  1L      33L
```

Strings

Split long strings on line boundaries. Line up the beginnings of each line.

```
/* A long string */

/* Help text */
static char *help = "\
F1 -- Display help text\n\
F2 -- Open new file\n\
F3 -- Close file\n\
F4 -- Change directory\n\
ESC -- Exit";
```

Statement Formatting

Write one statement per line.

```
/* Poor programming practice */
biggest=-1;first=0;count=57;init_key_words();
if(debug)open_log_files();table_size=parse_size+lex_size;


/* Much better */
biggest = -1;
first = 0;
count = 57;

init_key_words();

if (debug)
    open_log_files();

table_size = parse_size + lex_size;
```

Put spaces before and after each arithmetic operator.
Change long, complex statements into many smaller, simpler ones.

```
/* This is a big mess */
gain = (old_value - new_value) /
       (total_old - total_new) * 100.0;

/* Good practice */
delta_value = (old_value - new_value);
delta_total = (total_old - total_new);
gain = delta_value / delta_total * 100.0;
```

In a statement that consists of two or more lines, all lines that follow the first must be indented an extra level to show that they are continuations of the first line.

When writing multi-line statements, put the arithmetic and logical operators at the end of each line.

```
/* Bad */
net_profit = gross_profit - overhead
- cost_of_goods - payroll;

/* Good */
net_profit = gross_profit - overhead -
        cost_of_goods - payroll;
```

When breaking up a line, the preferred split point is where the parenthetic nesting is lowest.

Align like level parentheses vertically.

```
/* Don't program like this */
result = (((x1 + 1) * (x1 + 1)) -
        ((y1 + 1) * (y1 + 1)));

/* Program like this */
result = (((x1 + 1) * (x1 + 1)) -
        ((y1 + 1) * (y1 + 1)));

/* Same statement with
 * parentheses numbered for illustration */
```

$$\text{result} = (_1(_2(_3x1 + 1)_3 * (_3x1 + 1)_3)_2 -$$
$$(_2(_3y1 + 1)_3 * (_3y1 + 1)_3)_2)_1;$$

For Statements

Split long **for** statements along statement boundaries.
Always split a **for** statement into three lines.

```
for (index = start;
    data[index] != 0;
    index++)


/* Poor practice */
for (index = start; data[index] != 0;
    index++)
```

Switch Statements

Write **switch** statements on a single line.

```
/* Bad practice */
    switch (state_list[cur_state].next_state +
            goto_list[last_last] +
            special_overrides) {

/* Good practice */
    switch_index =  (state_list[cur_state].next_state +
                    goto_list[last_last] +
                    special_overrides);
    switch (switch_index) {
```

Conditionals

Keep conditionals on a single line if possible.

```
/* Good practice */
status_string = (status == GOOD) ? "Good" : "Bad";
```

When splitting up a conditional clause (? :), write it on three lines: the condition line, the true-value line, and the false-value line. Indent the last two lines an extra level.

```
/* OK practice */
status_string = (status == GOOD) ?
                            "Good" :
                            "Bad";
```

Side Effects

Avoid side effects.

Put the operators ++ and -- on lines by themselves. Do not use ++ and -- inside other statements.

```
/* Bad practice */
*destination++ = *source++;
```

```
/* Good practice */
*destination = *source;
destination++;
source++;
```

Never put an assignment statement inside any other statement.

```
/* Bad practice */
if ((ch = getch()) != EOF)
```

```
/* Good practice */
ch = getch();
if (ch != EOF)
```

When to Put Two Statements per Line

If putting two or more statements on a single line clarifies the program, then do so.

When using more than one statement per line, organize the statements into columns.

```
/* Not as clear as it can be */

    token[0].word = "if";
    token[0].value = TOKEN_IF;
    token[1].word = "while";
    token[1].value = TOKEN_WHILE;

    token[2].word = "switch";
    token[2].value = TOKEN_SWITCH;

    token[3].word = "case";
    token[3].value = TOKEN_CASE;

/* Clearer */
    token[0].word = "if";      token[0].value = TOKEN_IF;
    token[1].word = "while";   token[1].value = TOKEN_WHILE;
    token[2].word = "switch";  token[2].value = TOKEN_SWITCH;
    token[3].word = "case";    token[3].value = TOKEN_CASE;
```

Indentation

Indent one level for each new level of logic.

The best indentation size is four spaces.

```
while (count > 0) {
    if (balance[index] == EOF_MARKER)
        count = -1;
    else
        total += balance[index];
    index++;
}
```

Null Statement

Always put a comment in the null statement, even if it is only /* *Do Nothing* */.

```
/* Bad practice */
        for (i = 0; string[i] != 'x'; i++);
```

```
/* Good practice */
        for (i = 0; string[i] != 'x'; i++)
                /* Do nothing */;
```

Expressions

In C expressions you can assume that *, /, and % come before + and -. Put parentheses around everything else.

```
/* Good practice */
good_status = (status_byte & (1 << ERROR_BIT)) == 0);
```

Function Declarations

Use ANSI style function declarations whenever possible.

```
/* Preferred */
int function(int start, int middle, float average)

/* Use only when the compiler forces you to */
int function(start, middle, average)
int start;
int middle;
float average;
```

Always declare a function type.

```
/* Poor practice */
function(int start, int middle, float average)
```

Always declare functions that do not return a value void.
Allow no more than five parameters to a function.
When using K&R parameters, declare a type for every parameter.

```
/* Poor practice */
int function(start, middle, average)
float average;
```

When using K&R parameters, put the type declarations for the parameters in the same order as they occur in the function header.

```
/* Confusing */
int function(start, middle, average)
float average;

int start;
int middle;

/*Better*/
int function (start, middle, average)
int start;
int middle;
float average;
```

Avoid using global variables where function parameters will do.

```
/* Poor practice */
void get_token(void)
        /* Returns next token in global "token" */

/* Better */
void get_token(token_type *token_we_just_got)
```

Avoid variable length parameter lists. They are difficult to program and can easily cause trouble.

If Statements

When an **if** affects more than one line, enclose the target in braces.

```
/* Poor practice */
if (need_scan)
    for (i = 0; line[i] != ' '; i++)
        if (line[i] == 'x')
            x_count++;
```

```
/* Good practice */
if (need_scan) {
    for (i = 0; line[i] != ' '; i++) {
        if (line[i] == 'x')
            x_count++;
    }
}
```

In an **if** chain, treat the words **else if** as one keyword.

```
/* Poor practice */
if (strcmp(command, "open") == 0)
    do_open();
else if (strcmp(command, "close") == 0)
        do_close();
    else if (strcmp(command, "release") == 0)
            do_release();
        else
            do_unknown();
```

```
/* Good practice */
if (strcmp(command, "open") == 0)
    do_open();
else if (strcmp(command, "close") == 0)
    do_close();
else if (strcmp(command, "release") == 0)
    do_release();
else
    do_unknown();
```

The Comma Operator

Never use the comma operator when you can use braces instead.

```
/* Poor practice */
if (reset)
    line_count = 0, total = 0;
```

```
/* Good practice */
if (reset) {
    line_count = 0;
    total = 0;
}
```

Infinite Loops

When looping forever, use *while (1)* instead of *for(;;)*.

```
/* Poor practice */
for (;;) {
    /* .... */

/* Good practice */
while (1) {
    /* .... */
```

Do/While Statements

Avoid **do/while**. Use **while** and **break** instead.

```
/* Poor practice */
do {
    ch = getch()
} while (ch != EOF);

/* Good practice */
while (1) {
    ch = getch();
    if (ch == EOF)
        break;
}
```

For Statements and the Comma Operator

Use the comma operator inside a **for** statement only to put together two statements. Never use it to combine three statements.

Goto Statement

Start **goto** labels in the first column.

```
for (x = X_START; x < X_END; x++) {
    for (y = Y_START; y < Y_END; y++) {
        if (screen[x][y] == look_for)

                goto found_it;
    }
}
fprintf(stderr,"Not found\n");
return;


found_it:
    fprintf(stderr, "Found at (%d,%d)\n", x, y);
```

Switch Statements

End every **case** in a **switch** with a **break** or the comment /* *Fall Through* */.

Always put a **break** at the end of the last **case** in a **switch** statement.

Always include a **default** case in every **switch**, even if it consists of nothing but a null statement.

```
/* Good style */
switch (state) {
    case BEGIN_STATE:
        printf("Beginning\n");
        /* Fall Through */
    case PROC_STATE:
        printf("Processing\n");
        break;
    case FINISH_STATE:
        printf("Finishing\n");
        break;
    default:
        fprintf(stderr,
            "Internal error. Impossible state %d\n",
            state);
        exit (1);
}
```

Printf Statements

When possible, use one *printf* for each line of output.

```
/* Poor practice (printf writes 2 lines) */
printf("Start=%d\nEnd=%d\n", start, end);

/* Good practice */
printf("Start=%d\n", start);
printf("End=%d\n", end);

/* Poor practice (Printf write 1/2 line) */
printf("Start");
printf("=%d\n", start);
```

Unless extreme efficiency is warranted, use *printf* instead of *puts* and *putc*.

Begin each temporary debug *printf* with the characters ##. It readily identifies the output as debug chatter and makes it easy to remove the debug statements with your editor.

Shut up Statements

Your program should generate as few warnings as possible. Shut up statements can eliminate some of these.

```
/* Our copyright */
static char *copyright = "Copyright 1992 Steve Oualline";

main()
{
    (void)copyright; /* Avoid warning */

    /*
     *(Eliminates the "variable copyright not used"
     *  warning
     */
```

The Preprocessor

#define constants are declared like variables. Always put a comment that describes the constant after each declaration.

Constant names are all upper-case.

```
#define ENTRY_MAX     100      /* Maximum number of entries */
#define BLANK_X       30       /* X location (pixels) for blank */
```

If the value of a constant is anything other than a single number, enclose it in parentheses.

```
#define SIMPLE        5        /* OK, simple number */
#define BOTH      5 + 8        /* Bad, expression needs () */
#define GOOD      (5 + 8)      /* Good, () in place */
```

The use of **const** is preferred over **#define** for specifying constants.

```
/* Poor practice */
#define LIMIT 100             /* Largest acceptable value */

/* Preferred */
const int limit = 100;        /* Largest acceptable value */
```

When possible, use **typedef** instead of **#define**.

```
/* Poor, can cause trouble */
#define STRING char *

/* Good, avoids trouble */
typedef char *string;
```

Don't use **#define** to define new language elements.

```
/* Poor practice */
#define BEGIN {
#define END }

/* ... */
    if (x == y) BEGIN
        move_cursor(x,y);
        paint_screen();
    END;
        /* Is this C? */
```

Never use **#define** to redefine C keywords or standard functions.

```
/* Poor practice */
#define strdup(str)          better_strdup(str)
```

Enclose parameterized macros in parentheses.
Enclose each argument to a parameterized macro in parentheses.

```
/* Bad, dangerous */
#define square(x) x * x

/* Bad, still dangerous */
#define square(x) (x * x)

/* Good, much safer */
#define square(x) ((x) * (x))
```

Always enclose macros that define multiple C statements in braces.

If a macro contains more than one statement, use the **do/while** trick to enclose the macro. (Don't forget to leave *out* the semicolon of the statement).

When creating multi-line macros, align the continuation characters (backslash \) in a column.

```
/* Good practice */
#define abort(reason)                                      \
    do {
                                                           \
        fprintf(log_file, "Abort: %s\n", reason);          \
        exit (1);
                                                           \
    } while (0);
```

Always comment like functions any parameterized macros that look like functions.

#include directives come just after the heading comments. Put system includes first, followed by local includes.

```
/**************
 *  Heading   *
 **************/
#include <stdio.h>
#include "local.h"
```

Do not use absolute paths in **#include** directives. Let the -*I* compile option do the work.

```
/* Poor practice */
#include "Y:\DEVELOP\SOURCE\HEADERS\NAMES.H"

/* Better */
#include "names.h"
        /* Compile with -IY:\DEVELOP\SOURCE\HEADERS */
```

Comment **#else** and **#endif** directives with the symbol used in the initial **#ifdef** or **#ifndef** directive.

```
/* Poor practice */
#ifdef DEBUG
    printf("Processing %d\n", record);
#endif
```

```
/* Better */
#ifdef DEBUG
    printf("Processing %d\n", record);
#endif DEBUG

/* Note, some nasty compilers force you to use: */
#ifdef DEBUG
    printf("Processing %d\n", record);
#endif /* DEBUG */
```

Use conditional compilation sparingly. Don't let the conditionals obscure the code.

Define (or undefine) conditional compilation control symbols in the code rather than as a *-D* option to the compiler.

Put the **#define** and **#undef** statements for compilation control symbols at the beginning of the program.

```
#undef CHECK  /* Turn off internal checks */
#define DEBUG /* Turn on debugging output */
/**************
 *  Heading   *
 **************/
```

Do not comment out code. Use conditional compilation (*#ifdef UNDEF*) to get rid of unwanted code.

```
/* Poor practice (causes trouble) */
/*------ removed for debugging ----
delete(old_output);  /* Get rid of old output */
start_part_2();
 *------ end of section removed for debugging ---- */

#ifdef UNDEF
delete(old_output);  /* Get rid of old output */
start_part_2();
#endif UNDEF
```

Use *#ifdef QQQ* to temporarily eliminate code during debugging.

```
/* Maybe we'll learn something if we take this out */
#ifdef QQQ
    recalculate();
#endif QQQ
```

C++ Style

Use C style comments (/* .. */) for multi-line comments. Use C++ comments (//) for single-line comments.

```
//**********************************************
// This type of multi-line comment is awkward  *
// because we must begin each line with //.     *
// Not only that, but it looks funny.           *
//**********************************************


/**********************************************
 * Using traditional C comments for boxes like  *
 * this looks nicer and is not as awkward.      *
 **********************************************/

/* This code is broken  (total not defined) */
int count;      /* Number of items seen so far
int total;      /* Cost of all items */

// This code works
int count;      // Number of items seen so far
int total;      // Cost of all items
```

Do not put function bodies inside a class declaration. Use a function prototype in the class with a one-line comment. Put the full function body (**inline**) functions or fully comment prototype in the header following the class.

Put the function declarations for a class immediately after the class.

Always start a class declaration with the keyword **public**, **private**, or **protected**. Don't depend on defaults.

Always declare a constructor, destructor, copy and assignment function. If the C++ default is used, these declarations can be just a comment.

Avoid nested class, structure, and union definitions.

```
// Good class
class stack {
    private:
        int data[STACK_MAX];    // Data in the stack
        int current_index;      // Index into the stack
    public:
        stack(void);            // Create a stack
        // ~stack(void);        // Use default destructor

            // Use default copy function
        // stack(const stack &s);

        // Use default assignment
        // void operator = (const stack &s)

        // Push a new element on the stack
        void push(int value);

        // Pop top element off the stack
        int pop(void);
};

// ... function definitions
```

A function in a derived class that overrides a base class function must be commented: *"This function overrides the base class."*

The functions *setjmp* and *longjmp* can cause big problems because they skip the normal destruction process at the end of a procedure. Do not use them in functions that use classes.

When overloading a function, each flavor of the function should perform the same general operation.

```
// This is OK
int inline max(int i1, int i2)
{
    if (i1 > i2)
        return (i1);
    return (i2);
}
// This is OK too
float inline max(float f1, float f2)
{
    if (f1 > f2)
        return (f1);
    return (f2);
}
// This is bad
int inline max(int i1, int i2, int i3)
{
        return (i1 + i2 + i3);
}
```

Overload operators only if the operation makes sense.

Choose one I/O package for your program and stick to it.

Makefile Standards

Whenever possible, put all the files for one program in one directory.

The comment in a *Makefile* must describe the program, all the targets, and any configuration information needed by the programmer.

```
###############################################################
# Makefile for creating the program "hello"    #
# Set the variable SYSTEM to the               #
# appropriate value for your                   #
#       operating system.                      #
#                                              #
# Targets are:                                 #
#       all -- create the program "hello"      #
#       clean -- remove all object files       #
```

```
#        clobber -- same as clean                    #
#        install -- put the program in               #
#                          /usr/local/bin            #
#                                                     #
# SYSTEM=-DBSD4_3  For Berkeley UNIX Version 4.3      #
# SYSTEM=-DSYSV    For AT&T System V UNIX             #
# SYSTEM=-DSCO     For SCO UNIX                       #
# SYSTEM=-DDOS     For DOS (Borland Turbo C)          #
#####################################################
```

Standard targets are:

all

> Compiles all the programs. This is the standard default target.

install

> Copies files into the installation directory.

clean

> Removes all program binaries and object files.

clobber

> Like *clean*, this target removes all derived files.

lint (UNIX systems)

> Run the source files through the program checker *lint*.

Other, less common targets include:

depend or *maketd*

> Create a list of dependencies automatically.

srcs

> Checks out the sources from a software control system such as *SCCS* or *RCS*.

print

    Prints the sources on the line printer.

xrf

    Creates a cross reference printout.

debug

    Compiles the program with the debug flag enabled.

shar

    Makes a shar format archive.

Standard *Makefile* variables are:

CC

    The C compiler.

CFLAGS

    Flags supplied to the C compiler for compiling a single module.

LDFLAGS

    Flags supplied to the C compiler for loading all the objects into a single program.

SRCS or *SOURCES*

    The list of source files.

OBJS or *OBJECTS*

    The list of object files.

HDRS or *HEADER*

    The list of header files.

DESTDIR

    The destination directory, where the "install" target puts the files.

User-Friendly Programming

The Law of Least Astonishment:The program should behave in a way that least astonishes the user.

Programmer-Friendly Programming

Make your program as clear and easy to understand as possible. We need all the help we can get.

Examples

This section contains several examples from real programs. These examples are set out with the code on the left hand page and the comments, where applicable, on the facing page. The examples include:

- A small, one file program to count words (*wcount.c*)
- A C module for infinite arrays (*ia.h* and *ia.c*)
- A C++version of the same module (*ia.h* and *ia.c*)

File: wcount.c

This is a short single file program designed to count the number of characters, words, or lines in a file. It is included to demonstrate some of the style elements for program design.

```
/******************************************************** <note 1>
 *   wcount — count characters/words/lines in files       *
 *                                                         *
 * Usage:                                                  *
 *       wcount [-v] [files]                                *
 *                                                         *
 *       -v — print number of words in quotes vs            *
 *              outside of quotes                           *
 *       [files] — list of files to check                   *
 *              (No files, used standard in)                *
 *                                                         *
 * Based on the UNIX command "wc", but is much more         *
 * verbose.                                                 *
 ********************************************************/
#include <stdio.h>
#include <stdlib.h>
#include <string.h>

typedef int boolean;    /* Default a boolean type */ <note 2>
const TRUE = 1;         /* Values for boolean type */ <note 3>
const FALSE = 0;

<note 4>
static long     line_count; /* number of lines for this file */
static long     word_count; /* number of words for this file */

/* number of chars for this file */
static long     character_count;    static long

long_line_length;            /* length of longest line */

/* line number of longest line */
static long     long_line_number;
```

Note 1:

> The heading comments are short. Only what's needed is included. This is a personal program, so the author and copyright are unnecessary. Care must be taken to make everything in the heading comment relevant. Irrelevant information take time to maintain. Also most programmers finding updating excess information a chore, and too often skip doing it.

Note 2:

> **typedef** is used instcad of **#define**.

Note 3:

> **const** is used instead of **#define**.

Note 4:

> This program counts lines, words, and characters. Each of these counters ends with the suffix *_count*.

<note 5>

```
static long total_line_count; /* number of lines for all files */
static long total_word_count; /* number of words for all files */
static long total_character_count; /* number of chars all files */
static long total_long_line_length;/* length of longest line */
static long total_long_line_number;/* line number of longest ln */
static char *long_file_name;        /* name of the long file */

/* number of words outside/inside quotes */
static long     quote_words[2];

static boolean in_quote;        /* True if we are inside a quote */

/* True if we are to count quote/not quote */
static boolean verbose = FALSE;
```

<note 6>

```
/**********************************************************
 * w_print — Print statistics                            *
 *                                                        *
 * Parameters                                             *
 *      print_character_count — number of chars to        *
 *                              print                     *
 *      print_word_count — number of words to print       *
 *      print_line_count — number of line to print        *
 *      print_long_line_length — Lengths of longest        *
 *                              line in the source file *
 *      print_long_line_number — line number of the        *
 *                  longest line                          *
 *      file_name — name of the file to print             *
 *           (OR NULL for no file)                        *
 **********************************************************/
static void w_print(long print_character_count,
                long print_word_count,
                long print_line_count,
                long print_long_line_length,
                long print_long_line_number,
                char *file_name)
```

Note 5:

The program keeps two sets of running totals: one for the current file and one for all files. Notice that the variables for the "all file" counters begin with the prefix *total_*. Also, these the "all file" variables are intentionally declared in the same order as the "single file" variables.

(When writing the program we produced the second section by copying the first and adding the word *total_* before each name.)

Note 6:

The function *w_print* takes 6 parameters. This is about the limit for functions. You can see the difficulty we had with this function.

```
    {
        printf(
    " chars:%ld, words:%ld, lines:%ld, longest line:%ld at %ld ",
                print_character_count,
                print_word_count,
                print_line_count,
                print_long_line_length,
                print_long_line_number);

        if (file_name != NULL)
            printf(" in file %s\n", file_name);

        printf("\n");
    }


main(int argc, char *argv[])
{
    register char old_c;   /* Previous character */
    int cur_file;          /* Index into argv[] for this file */
    boolean in_word;       /* True if we are inside a word */
    register FILE *in_file;   /* File we are reading */
    register int c;           /* Current character */
    register int line_length; /* Length of this line */

    cur_file = 1;
    in_file = stdin;
```

\<note 7\>

```
    /*
     * Check for a "-v" (verbose) option
     */
    if ((argc > 1) && (strcmp(argv[1],"-v") == 0)) {
        verbose = TRUE;
        argv++;
        argc—;
    }

    while (1) {
        if (argc > 1) {
            in_file=fopen(argv[cur_file], "r");
```

Note 7:

Notice that the program is divided into sections each beginning with a multi-line comment.

```
        if (in_file == NULL) {
            perror(argv[cur_file]);
            continue;
        }
    }
    /*
     * Reset all counters
     */
    line_count = 0;
    word_count = 0;
    character_count = 0;
    in_word = 0;
    line_length = 0;
    long_line_number = -1;
    long_line_length = -1;
    in_quote = FALSE;
    quote_words[0] = 0;
    quote_words[1] = 0;

    c = -1;

    /*
     * Loop for each line
     */
    while (1) {
        old_c = c;
        c = getc(in_file);
        if (c == EOF)
            break;

        character_count++;

        if (c == '\"')
            in_quote = ! in_quote;

        if ((c == '\n') && (old_c == '\n'))
            in_quote = FALSE;
```

EXAMPLES

```
    /*
     * Add to line length if a printing character
     */
    if (c >= ' ') {
        line_length++;
    }

    if (' '<c) {
        if(!in_word) {
            word_count++;
            quote_words[in_quote]++;
            in_word = TRUE;
        }
        continue;
    }

    if(c=='\n') {
        if (line_length > long_line_length) {
            long_line_number = line_count;
            long_line_length = line_length;
        }
        line_length = 0;
        line_count++;
    } else {
        if ((c!=' ') && (c!='\t'))
            continue;
    }
    in_word = FALSE;
}
if(argc>1)
    printf(" %s: ", argv[cur_file]);

/* print lines, words, chars */
w_print(character_count, word_count, line_count,
        long_line_length, long_line_number, NULL);
```

EXAMPLES

```
                if (verbose)
                        printf(  <note 8>
    "
        In quotes %ld, Outside %ld  %%Quoted %2.1f\n",
                quote_words[1], quote_words[0],
                (float)quote_words[1] /
                        ((float)quote_words[1]
                            + (float)quote_words[0]) *100.0);
        fclose(in_file);

        /*
         * Add current file information to totals
         */

        total_line_count += line_count;
        total_word_count += word_count;
        total_character_count += character_count;

        if (total_long_line_length < long_line_length) {
                total_long_line_length = long_line_length;
                total_long_line_number = long_line_number;
                long_file_name = argv[cur_file];
        }
        cur_file++;
        if (cur_file >= argc)
            break;
    }
    /*
     * Print totals if more than one file
     */
    if(argc > 2) {
        printf(" total: ");
        w_print(total_character_count,
                total_word_count,
                total_line_count,
                long_line_length,
                long_line_number,
                long_file_name);
    }
    return (0);
}
```

Note 8:

> The string for this line is too long to fit on the page when properly indented. There should be a good solution to this problem, but we don't know what it is, so by default we've indented it as much as possible.

File: ia.h

This is an example of a simple module. It provides a general-purpose "infinite array," an array in which the programmer can store any number of elements (as long as there is memory left).

```
/************************************************************
 * Infinite Array — This package defines operations        *
 *      for "infinite arrays." These arrays grow as        *
 *      needed.                                            *
 *                                                        *
 * Author:    Steve Oualline                              *
 *                                                        *
 * Assumptions:                                           *
 *      This implementation assumes that the elements     *
 *      being stored are pointers.                        *
 *                                                        *
 * Functions:                                   <note 1> *
 *      IaInit — create an infinite array.                *
 *      IaGet(ia, index) — get an element from an         *
 *                       array.                           *
 *      IaPut(ia, index, data) — store element            *
 *      IaFree(ia) — destroy an infinite array.           *
 *                                                        *
 * Notes: This package is begging to be written in C++    *
 ************************************************************/
const bucket 50        /* Size of each bucket */ <note 2>

/* <note 3>
 * Structure for an infinite array.  The actual
 * array is one or more of these segments
 */
struct ia {
    /* The data we are storing in this bucket */ <note 4>
    void *data[bucket];

    struct ia *next;     /* Pointer to next bucket */
};
typedef struct ia IA; <note 5>
```

Note 1:

Normally we don't include a list of functions in the comment headings. We have included one for this package because the number of functions is fixed (not expected to grow) and small (only four functions). Because of this, a list is easy to add and maintain and a correct function list is somewhat useful. We've decided to use the common prefix *Ia* for all the functions in this package.

Note 2:

const is preferred over **#define.**

Note 3:

We've put a comment at the beginning of the structure as well as commenting each filed.

Note 4:

This comment is too long to put at the end of the line, so it goes above the declaration.

Note 5:

We're using **typedef** to define a new type. Note that the name of the type (IA) and the name of the structure (ia) are the same, except for case. This gives us a good correspondence between the names.

<note 6>

```
/**************************************************
 * IaInit — create an infinite array              *
 *                                                 *
 * Returns                                         *
 *       new, empty infinite array                 *
 **************************************************/
IA *IaInit(void);


/**************************************************
 * IaGet — get an element from the array          *
 *                                                 *
 * Parameters                                      *
 *       ia — the infinite array                   *
 *       index — index of the element we want      *
 *                                                 *
 * Returns                                         *
 *       element or NULL for uninitialized elements *
 **************************************************/
void *IaGet(IA *ia, int index);


/**************************************************
 * IaPut — store an element in an array           *
 *                                                 *
 * Parameters                                      *
 *       ia — the infinite array                   *
 *       index — index of the element to store     *
 *       data — data to store                      *
 **************************************************/
void IaPut(IA *ia, int index, void *data);


/**************************************************
 * IaFree — destroy an infinite array             *
 *                                                 *
 * Parameters                                      *
 *       ia — the array to destroy                 *
 **************************************************/
void IaFree(IA *ia);
```

Note 6:

A list of function prototypes follows. Each prototype is commented just like the real functions. In fact, we used *cut* and *paste* to copy these function headings from the file *ia.c*.

File ia.c

This file contains code for the infinite array module. The public part of the module has already been described by the file *ia.h*. This file contains the private part of the module, the section that really does the work.

```
/***********************************************************
 * Infinite Array — This package defines operations <note 1>*
 *      for "infinite arrays."  These arrays grow as    *
 *      needed.                                         *
 *                                                      *
 * This implementation assumes that the elements        *
 * being stored are pointers.                           *
 *                                                      *
 * Functions:                                           *
 *      IaInit — create an infinite array.              *
 *      IaGet(ia, index) — get an element from an       *
 *                      array.                          *
 *      IaPut(ia, index, data) — store element          *
 *      IaFree(ia) — destroy an infinite array.         *
 *                                                      *
 * Notes: This package is begging to be written in C++  *
 ***********************************************************/
#ifdef __TURBOC__  <note 2>
#include <alloc.h>
#include <mem.h>
#include <process.h>
#else /* __TURBOC__ */
#include <stdlib.h>     /* Watcom */
#include <string.h>     /* Watcom puts memset here */ <note 3>
#endif /* __TURBOC__ */
```

Note 1:

These heading comments are the same as the ones in *ia.h*.

Note 2:

This package compiles under two different C compilers: Borland C and WATCOM. Each compiler puts the prototype for *memset* in a different file. We've overcome this problem through conditional compilation.

We've decided to use the symbol _ _*TURBOC*_ _ for our condition because it is automatically generated by Borland C. We've decided to use a compiler defined symbol instead of one we defined ourselves so that the conditional is invoked without having to do any work.

Note 3:

A reasonable person wouldn't expect the function memset to be in the header file *string.h*. But that's where WATCOM puts it. We've included a comment documenting this astonishing fact.

```
#include <stdio.h>
#include "ia.h"          <note 4>

<note 5>
/***********************************************************
 * z_malloc — malloc zeroed memory                         *
 *        (Like malloc, but clears the memory and checks   *
 *         for errors.)                                    *
 *                                                         *
 * Parameters                                              *
 *     size — the number of bytes to allocate              *
 *                                                         *
 * Returns                                                 *
 *     pointer to new data                                 *
 ***********************************************************/
static void *z_malloc(unsigned int size)
{
    void *new_ptr;        /* New data from malloc */

    new_ptr = z_malloc(size);


    if (new_ptr == NULL) {
        fprintf(stderr,"Error: Out of memory\n");
        exit(1);
    }

    memset(new_ptr, '\0', size);
    return (new_ptr);
}
/***********************************************************
 * IaInit — create an infinite array                       *
 *                                                         *
 * Returns                                                 *
 *     new, empty infinite array                           *
 ***********************************************************/
IA *IaInit(void)
{
    return(z_malloc(sizeof(IA)));
}
```

Note 4:

> We always include the module header file in the module, even if it's not necessary in order for the program to work. This causes the compiler to check the prototypes in the header file against the actual functions. (Also, if we always include the header, we don't have to worry about whether or not it is necessary.)

Note 5:

> We've defined a better version of the *malloc* function. Rather than redefine the existing library function, we've called ours *z_malloc*. This name makes it obvious that this function looks and acts a lot like *malloc*.

<note 6>

```
/************************************************************
 * ia_find — locate an element in the array                 *
 *                                                          *
 * Parameters                                               *
 *      ia — the array to look through                      *
 *      index — the index to look for                       *
 *                                                          *
 * Returns                                                  *
 *      pointer to the element                              *
 ************************************************************/
static void **ia_find(IA *ia, int index)
{
    while (index >= bucket) {
        if (ia->next == NULL) {
            ia->next = z_malloc(sizeof(IA));
        }
        ia = ia->next;
        index -= bucket;
    }
    return (&ia->data[index]);
}
/************************************************************
 * IaGet — get an element from the array                    *
 *                                                          *
 * Parameters                                               *
 *      ia — the infinite array                             *
 *      index — index of the element we want                *
 *                                                          *
 * Returns                                                  *
 *      element or NULL for uninitialized elements          *
 ************************************************************/
void *IaGet(IA *ia, int index)
{
    void **element_ptr;

    element_ptr = ia_find(ia, index);
    return (*element_ptr);
}
```

Note 6:

Our function *InaInit* could have just as easily been a macro

```
/***********************************************************
 * IaPut — store an element in an array                    *
 *                                                         *
 * Parameters                                              *
 *       ia — the infinite array                           *
 *       index — index of the element to store             *
 *       data — data to store                              *
 ***********************************************************/
void IaPut(IA *ia, int index, void *data)
{
    void **element_ptr;

    element_ptr = ia_find(ia, index);
    *element_ptr = data;
}


/***********************************************************
 * IaFree — destroy an infinite array                      *
 *                                                         *
 * Parameters                                              *
 *       ia — the array to destroy                         *
 ***********************************************************/
void IaFree(IA *ia)
{
    IA *next;

    while (ia != NULL) {
        next = ia->next;
        SafeFree(ia);
        ia = next;
    }
}
```

File ia2.h

We already said that our "infinite array" package was begging to be written in C++. We've done that, producing an infinite array class that can be treated much like an array.

```
/************************************************************
 * class IA — an infinite array class                     *
 *                                                         *
 * This implementation assumes that the elements           *
 * being stored are pointers.  (This could be made         *
 * into a template and store anything.)                    *
 ************************************************************/
```

```
// Single of a bucket for IA   (private to IA)
const ia_bucket_size = 50;
```

<note 1>
```
/*
 * A bucket to put data for an infinite array
 * (Private to the IA class)
 */
struct ia_bucket {
    void *data[ia_bucket_size];// Data
    struct ia_bucket *next;    // Pointer to next bucket
};
```

```
class IA {
    private: <note 2>
        struct ia_bucket *first;// Pointer to first bucket

    public:          <note 3>
        IA(void);        // Create the infinite array
        ~IA(void);       // destroy the infinite array
        IA(IA &old);     // copy operator
        IA &operator = (const IA &old); // assignment operator

        // get/set an element in the array
        void * &operator[](const int index);
};
```

Note 1:

This structure is private to the **class** *IA*. It was defined here instead of inside the **class** *IA* to simplify the class definition.

Note 2:

We explicitly declare everything **public** or **private**. The default is not used.

Note 3:

Here we define short versions of each procedure. Longer versions will follow in this header file.

```
/***********************************************************
 * IA::IA - create an infinite array                       *
 ***********************************************************/
inline IA::IA(void)
{
    first = new ia_bucket;
}


/***********************************************************
 * IA &operator =   (Infinite array assignment operator) *
 *                                                         *
 * Not allowed.                                            *
 ***********************************************************/
#pragma warn -rvl
IA inline &IA::operator = (const IA &old)
{
    (void)old;  // Avoid warning
    fprintf(stderr,
        "Assignment operator not allowed for IAs\n");
    exit (8);
}
#pragma warn .rvl
/***********************************************************
 * IA::IA(IA &old) - copy operation                        *
 *                                                         *
 * Not allowed.                                            *
 ***********************************************************/
inline IA::IA(IA &old)
{
    (void)old;  // Avoid warning
    fprintf(stderr,"Copy operation not allowed for IAs\n");
    exit (8);
}
/***********************************************************
 * IA::operator[] - point to an item in the array          *
 *                                                         *
 * Parameters                                              *
 *      index - index of the element to refer to     *
 ***********************************************************/
void * &IA::operator[](const int index);
```

File ia2.cpp

This file contains the CC++ implementation of the infinite array package.

```
/***********************************************************
 * class IA - an infinite array class                     *
 *                                                         *
 * This implementation assumes that the elements           *
 * being stored are pointers.  (This could be made         *
 * into a template and store anything.)                    *
 ***********************************************************/
#include <stdio.h>
#include <stdlib.h>
#include "ia2.h"

/***********************************************************
 * IA::~IA -- destroy the infinite array                  *
 ***********************************************************/
IA::~IA(void) {
    struct ia_bucket *current;  // Bucket we are killing
    struct ia_bucket *next;     // next bucket on the list

    current = first;
    while (current != NULL) {
        next = current->next;
        delete current;
        current = next;
    }
}


/***********************************************************
 * IA::operator[] -- point to an item in the array        *
 *                                                         *
 * Parameters                                              *
 *      index -- index of the element to refer to          *
 ***********************************************************/
void * &IA::operator[](const int index)
{
    struct ia_bucket *current;  // Current bucket
    int cur_index;              // Current index we are working with
```

```
    cur_index = index;

    current = first;
    while (cur_index > ia_bucket_size) {
        if (current->next == NULL) {
            current->next = new ia_bucket;
            current = current->next;
            current->next = NULL;
        }
        cur_index -= ia_bucket_size;
    }
    return (current->data[cur_index]);
}
```

List of Rules by Chapter

1. Style and Program Organization

1-1. Organize programs for readability, just as you would expect an author to organize a book.

1-2. Divide each module up into a public part (what's needed to use the module) and a private part (what's needed to get the job done). The public part goes into a *.h* file while the private part goes into a *.c* file.

1-3. Use white space to break a function into paragraphs.

1-4. Put each statement on a line by itself.

1-5. Avoid very long statements. Use two shorter statements instead.

2. File Basics, Comments, and Program Headings

2-1. Keep programs files to no longer than about 2,000 to 3,000 lines.

2-2. Keep all lines in your program files down to 72 characters or fewer.

2-3. Use 8-character tab stops.

2-4. Use only the 95 standard ASCII characters in your programming. Avoid exotic characters.

2-5. Include a heading comment at the beginning of each file that explains the file.

2-6. Leave out unnecessary comments if they require maintenance and if you are unlikely to maintain them.

2-7. Comment your code as you write it.

3. Variable Names

3-1. Use simple, descriptive variable names.

3-2. Good variable names can be created by using one word or by putting two or three words together, separated by an underscore (_).

3-3. Never use *l* (lower-case L) or *O* (upper-case O) as variable or constant names.

3-4. Don't use the names of existing C library functions or constants.

3-5. Don't use variable names that differ by only one or two characters. Variable names should be obviously different.

3-6. Use similar names for variables that perform similar functions.

3-7. When creating a two-word variable name where the words can be put in any order, always put the most important word first.

3-8. Standard prefixes and suffixes are *_ptr*, *_p*, *_file*, *_fd*, and *n_*.

3-9. Short names such as *x*, *y*, and *i* are acceptable when their meaning is clear and when a longer name would not add information or clarity.

3-10. Use *argc* for the number of command line arguments and *argv* for the argument list. Do not use these names for anything else.

3-11. Follow every variable declaration with a comment that defines it.

3-12. Whenever possible, include the units of measure in the description of a variable.

3-13. Name and comment each field in a structure or union like a variable.

3-14. Begin each structure or union definition with a multi-line comment that defines it.

3-15. Put at least one blank line before and after a structure or union definition.

3-16. When you can't put a descriptive comment at the end of a variable declaration, put it on a separate line above. Use blank lines to separate the declaration/comment pair from the rest of the code.

3-17. Group similar variables together. When possible, use the same structure for each group.

3-18. Don't use hidden variables.

3-19. Use the names *INT16*, *INT32*, *UINT16*, and *UINT32* for portable applications.

3-20. Floating-point numbers must have at least one digit on either side of the decimal point.

3-21. The exponent in a floating-point number must be a lower-case e. This is always followed by a sign.

3-22. Start hexadecimal number with *0x*. (Lower-case *x* only.)

3-23. Use upper-case *A* through *F* when constructing hexadecimal constants.

3-24. Long constants should end with an upper-case *L*.

4. Statement Formatting

4-1. Write one statement per line.

4-2. Put spaces before and after each arithmetic operator, just like you put spaces between words in English.

4-3. Change long, complex statements into many smaller, simpler ones.

4-4. In a statement that consists of two or more lines, every line except the first must be indented an extra level to show that they are continuations of the first line.

4-5. When writing multi-line statements, put the arithmetic and logical operators at the end of each line.

4-6. When breaking up a line, the preferred split point is where the parenthetic nesting is lowest.

4-7. Align like level parentheses vertically.

4-8. Split long **for** statements along statement boundaries.

4-9. Always split a **for** statement into three lines.

4-10. Write **switch** statements on a single line.

4-11. Keep conditionals on a single line if possible.

4-12. When splitting up a conditional clause (? :), write it on three lines: the condition line, the true-value line, and the false-value line. Indent the last two lines an extra level.

4-13. Avoid side effects.

4-14. Put the operators ++ and -- on lines by themselves. Do not use ++ and -- inside other statements.

4-15. Never put an assignment statement inside any other statement.

4-16. If putting two or more statements on a single line improves program clarity, then do so.

4-17. When using more than one statement per line, organize the statements into columns.

4-18. Indent one level for each new level of logic.

4-19. The best indentation size is four spaces.

5. Statement Details

5-1. Always put a comment in the null statement, even if it is only /* *Do Nothing* */.

5-2. In C expressions you can assume that *, /, and % come before + and -. Put parentheses around everything else.

5-3. Use ANSI style function declarations whenever possible.

5-4. When using K&R parameters, declare a type for every parameter.

5-5. When using K&R parameters, put the type declarations for the parameters in the same order as they occur in the function header.

5-6. Always declare a function type.

5-7. Always declare functions that do not return a value **void**.

5-8. Allow no more than five parameters to a function.

5-9. Avoid using global variables where function parameters will do.

5-10. Avoid variable length parameter lists. They are difficult to program and can easily cause trouble.

5-11. When an **if** affects more than one line, enclose the target in braces.

5-12. In an **if** chain, treat the words **else if** as one keyword.

5-13. Never use the comma operator when you can use braces instead.

5-14. When looping forever, use **while (1)** instead of **for (;;)**.

5-15. Avoid **do/while**. Use **while** and **break** instead.

5-16. Use the comma operator inside a **for** statement only to put together two statements. Never use it to combine three statements.

5-17. Use one *printf* per line of output.

5-18. Unless extreme efficiency is warranted, use *printf* instead of *puts* and *putc*.

5-19. Start **goto** labels in the first column.

5-20. End every **case** in a **switch** with a **break** or the comment */* Fall Through */*.

5-21. Always put a **break** at the end of the last **case** in a **switch** statement.

5-22. Always include a **default** case in every **switch**, even if it consists of nothing but a null statement.

6. The Preprocessor

6-1. **#define** constants are declared like variables. Always include a comment that describes the constant after each declaration.

6-2. Constant names are all upper-case.

6-3. If the value of a constant is anything other than a single number, enclose it in parentheses.

6-4. The use of **const** is preferred over **#define** for specifying constants.

6-5. When possible, use **typedef** instead of **#define**.

6-6. Don't use **#define** to define new language elements.

6-7. Never use **#define** to redefine C keywords or standard functions.

6-8. Enclose parameterized macros in parentheses.

6-9. Enclose each argument to a parameterized macro in parentheses.

6-10. Always enclose macros that define multiple C statements in braces.

6-11. If a macro contains more than one statement, use the **do/while** trick to enclose the macro. (Don't forget to leave *out* the semicolon of the statement).

6-12. When creating multi-line macros, align the backslash continuation characters (\) in a column.

6-13. Always comment any parameterized macros that look like functions.

6-14. **#include** directives come just after the heading comments. Put system includes first, followed by local includes.

6-15. Do not use absolute paths in #include directives. Let the *-I* compile option do the work.

6-16. Comment **#else** and **#endif** directives with the symbol used in the initial **#ifdef** or **#ifndef** directive.

6-17. Use conditional compilation sparingly. Don't let the conditionals obscure the code.

6-18. Define (or undefine) conditional compilation control symbols in the code rather than using the *-D* option to the compiler.

6-19. Put the **#define** and **#undef** statements for compilation control symbols at the beginning of the program.

6-20. Do not comment out code. Use conditional compilation (*#ifdef UNDEF*) to get rid of unwanted code.

6-21. Use *#ifdef QQQ* to temporarily eliminate code during debugging.

7. C++ Style

7-1. Use C style comments (/* .. */) for multi-line comments. Use C++ comments (//) for single-line comments.

7-2. Put the function declarations for a class immediately after the class.

7-3. Do not put function bodies inside a class declaration. Use a function prototype in the class with a one-line comment. Put the full-function body (**inline**) functions or fully comment prototype in the header following the class.

7-4. Always declare a constructor, destructor, copy and assignment function. If the C++ default is used, these declarations can be just a comment.

7-5. Always start a class declaration with the keyword **public**, **private**, or **protected**. Don't depend on defaults.

7-6. Avoid nested class, structure, and union definitions.

7-7. When a member function in a derived class overrides a similar function in the base class, include a comment that shows that this is intentional.

7-8. Whenever possible, initialize variables at declaration time.

7-9. Be extremely careful with *setjmp* and *longjmp* in C++. Do not use them in functions that declare classes.

7-10. When overloading a function, each flavor of the function should perform the same general operation.

7-11. Overload operators only if the operation makes sense.

7-12. Choose one I/O package for your program and stick to it.

8. Directory Organization and Makefile Style

8-1. Whenever possible, put all the files for one program in one directory.

9. User-Friendly Programming

9-1. Law of Least Astonishment: The program should act in a way that least astonishes the user.

9-2. Begin each error message with *Error:*. Begin each warning message with *Warning:*.

9-3. Don't let users do something stupid without warning them.

Index

H

I

A Library of Technical References
from M&T Books

C++ Components and Algorithms
by Scott Robert Ladd

It's true: experienced C programmers always need the kind of comprehensive tools that can help them develop and maintain powerful C++ applications. This excellent volume is where you can find them—all of them! Memory management, indexed files using B-Trees, mathematical programming, adaptive algorithms and more. The in-depth discussions and numerous source code examples are geared toward an understanding of C++'s inner workings. The programs and classes presented are compatible with various C++ compilers, making them valuable to a wide audience of C programmers. All source code included on disk in MC/PC-DOS format. Now you can C more than ever! 512 pp.

Book/Disk $39.95   #2276

Level: Advanced

Clean Coding in Borland C++
by Robert J. Traister

Novice to intermediate C and C++ programmers —this is *the* learning guide to Borland C++! Get clear, easy-to-understand explanations of Borland C++'s features and functions, plus complete coverage of the powerful tools included with it. Learn how to write clean, efficient Borland C++ code, develop Windows applications, debug, design and more! All source code is available on disk in MS/PC-DOS format. 336 pp.

Book $26.95   #2055

Book/Disk $36.95   #2071

Level: Beginning-Intermediate

A Library of Technical References
from M&T Books

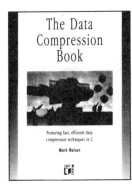

The Data Compression Book
by Mark Nelson

An authoritative guide for advanced C programmers. Details various data compression techniques, explaining the theory behind each and showing how to apply them to significantly increase your system's storage capacity. MS/PC-DOS disk contains sample source code. 527 pp.

Book	$29.95	#2144
Book/Disk	$39.95	#2160

Level: Advanced

Turbo C++ Techniques and Applications
by Scott Robert Ladd

Required reading for proficient C programmers moving to C++. Details Turbo C++ commands and functions, teaching programmers how to write code that fully utilizes the speed of Turbo C++. Covers Turbo Debugger and Tools, and Turbo Profiler. MS/PC-DOS disk contains sample source code. 423 pp.

Book	$29.95	#1474
Book/Disk	$39.95	#1466

Level: Intermediate

1-800-688-3987

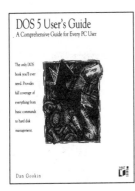

A Library of Technical References
from M&T Books

DOS 5: A Developer's Guide
Advanced Programming Guide to DOS
by Al Williams

Direct access techniques, fundamentals of graphics, expanded and extended memory, TSR programming, protected mode, and DOS extenders . . . this is the super guide to programming powerful, professional applications for all versions of MS-DOS! Solid examples plus the complete source code for an 80386 DOS extender. All of the source code is available on disk in MS/PC-DOS format. 914 pp.

Book	$34.95	#1776
Book/Disk	$39.95	#1792

Level: Advanced

DR DOS 6 By Example
by William F. Lawrence

The complete guide to using DR DOS 6, the operating system from Digital Research. Learn to install DR DOS 6, configure the system, and use its many features including ViewMax, DR DOS' graphical user interface. 534 pp.

Book	$26.95	#2454

Level: Beginning - Advanced

A Library of Technical References from M&T Books

Numerical Methods
by Don Morgan

Required reading for all assembly-language programmers. Contains the techniques needed to write mathematical routines for real-time embedded systems. Covers everything from data on the positional number system to algorithms for developing elementary functions. MS/PC-DOS disk contains sample source code. 512 pp.

Book/Disk	$36.95	#2322

Level: Advanced

A Small C Compiler, Second Edition
by James Hendrix

An excellent resource for programmers who want to learn the fundamentals of the C language. Thoroughly explains Small C's structure, syntax, and features, providing hands-on experience using C. Includes MS/PC-DOS disk containing fully-functional Small C compiler plus run-time library, source code, and executable assembler. 628 pp.

Book	$34.95	#1245

Level: Beginning

A Library of Technical References
from M&T Books

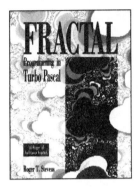

Fractal Programming in Turbo Pascal
by Roger T. Stevens

This book equips Turbo Pascal programmers with the tools needed to program dynamic fractal curves. It is a reference that gives full attention to developing the reader's understanding of various fractal curves. More than 100 black and white and 32 full-color fractals are illustrated throughout the book. All source code to reproduce the fractals is available on disks in MS/PC-DOS format. Requires a PC or clone with EGA or VGA, color monitor, and Turbo Pascal 4.0 or later. 462 pp.

Book	$29.95	#1067
Book/Disk (MS-DOS)	$39.95	#1075

Level: Intermediate

Advanced Fractal Programming in C
by Roger T. Stevens

Programmers who enjoyed our best-selling *Fractal Programming in C* can move on to the next level of fractal programming with this book. Included are how-to instructions for creating many different types of fractal curves, including source code. Contains 16 pages of full-color fractals. All the source code to generate the fractals is available on an optional disk in MS/PC-DOS format. 305 pp.

Book	$29.95	#0966
Book/Disk	$39.95	#0974

Level: Intermediate

1-800-688-3987

ORDER FORM

To Order:

Return this form with your payment to M&T Books, 411 Borel Avenue, Suite 100, San Mateo, CA 94402 or **call toll-free 1-800-533-4372 (in California, call 1-800-356-2002).**

ITEM #	DESCRIPTION	DISK	PRICE

Subtotal

CA residents add sales tax ____%

Add $4.50 per item for shipping and handling

TOTAL

Charge my:

☐ **Visa**

☐ **MasterCard**

☐ **AmExpress**

☐ **Check enclosed, payable to M&T Books.**

CARD NO.

SIGNATURE   EXP. DATE

NAME

ADDRESS

CITY

STATE   ZIP

M&T GUARANTEE: If your are not satisfied with your order for any reason, return it to us within 25 days of receipt for a full refund. Note: Refunds on disks apply only when returned with book within guarantee period. Disks damaged in transit or defective will be promptly replaced, but cannot be exchanged for a disk from a different title.

Tell us what you think and we'll send you a free M&T Books catalog

It is our goal at M&T Books to produce the best technical books available. But you can help us make our books even better by letting us know what you think about this particular title.Please take a moment to fill out this card and mail it to us. Your opinion is appreciated.

Tell us about yourself

Name_____

Company_____

Address_____

City_____

State/Zip_____

Title of this book?

_____

Where did you purchase this book?

☐ Bookstore
☐ Catalog
☐ Direct Mail
☐ Magazine Ad
☐ Postcard Pack
☐ Other

Why did you choose this book?

☐ Recommended
☐ Read book review
☐ Read ad/catalog copy
☐ Responded to a special offer
☐ M&T Books' reputation
☐ Price
☐ Nice Cover

How would you rate the overall content of this book?

☐ Excellent
☐ Good
☐ Fair
☐ Poor

Why?

_____

_____

What chapters did you find valuable?

_____

_____

_____

What did you find least useful?

_____

_____

_____

What topic(s) would you add to future editions of this book?

_____

_____

_____

What other titles would you like to see M&T Books publish?

_____

_____

_____

Which format do you prefer for the optional disk?

☐ 5.25"   ☐ 3.5"

Any other comments?

_____

_____

_____

☐ Check here for
M&T Books Catalog